Albanians in Michigan

19

DISCOVERING THE PEOPLES OF MICHIGAN
Arthur W. Helweg and Linwood H. Cousins, Series Editors

Ethnicity in Michigan: Issues and People
Jack Glazier, Arthur W. Helweg

French Canadians in Michigan
John P. DuLong

African Americans in Michigan
Lewis Walker, Benjamin C. Wilson, Linwood H. Cousins

Albanians in Michigan
Frances Trix

————————————————

Discovering the Peoples of Michigan is a series of publications examining the state's rich multicultural heritage. The series makes available an interesting, affordable, and varied collection of books that enables students and lay readers to explore Michigan's ethnic dynamics. A knowledge of the state's rapidly changing multicultural history has far-reaching implications for human relations, education, public policy, and planning. We believe that Discovering the Peoples of Michigan will enhance understanding of the unique contributions that diverse and often unrecognized communities have made to Michigan's history and culture.

Albanians in Michigan

Frances Trix

Michigan State University Press

East Lansing

⊚ The paper used in this publication meets the minimum requirements
of ANSI/NISO Z39.48-1992 (R 1997) (Permanence of Paper)

Michigan State University Press
East Lansing, Michigan 48823-5202
Printed and bound in the United States of America

07 06 05 04 03 02 01   1 2 3 4 5 6 7

LIBRARY OF CONGRESS CATALOGING-IN-PUBLICATION DATA
Trix, Frances.
Albanians in Michigan / Frances Trix.
p. cm. — (discovering the peoples of Michigan)
ISBN 0-87013-584-8 (alk. paper)
1. Albanian Americans—Michigan—History. 2. Albanian Americans—
Michigan—Social conditions. 3. Immigrants—Michigan—History. 4. Michigan—
Ethnic relations. 5. Michigan—Social conditions. I. Title. II. Series.
F575 .A3 T75 2001
305.891'9910774—dc21
2001002635

Discovering the People of Michigan. The editors wish
to thank the Kellogg Foundation for their generous support.

Cover design by Ariana Grabec-Dingman
Book design by Sharp Des!gns, Inc.

COVER PHOTO: Lula Shkreli and Peter Vuljaj, Wayne State University students
and members of the Albanian American Student Organization at Wayne State,
perform an Albanian dance. Photo by Mark P. Gjokaj.

Visit Michigan State University Press on the World Wide Web at:
www.msupress.msu.edu

ACKNOWLEDGMENTS

I would like to acknowledge leaders and members of the various Albanian communities in Michigan for their unfailing kindness and assistance to me over the long course of this project. For assistance with the earlier form of this project, I would like to thank Father Nicholas Liolin, Victor Chacho and wife Vivian, Ted Peppo, and Louis Dimitry of the Albanian Orthodox community; Father Prenk Ndrevashaj, Father Anton Kçira, Prenk Gruda, Albert Degaj, Mark P. Gjokaj, and Rrok Kalaj of the two Albanian Roman Catholic communities; Imam Vehbi Ismail, Baba Rexheb, Dervish Arshi, Shije Orhan Shahin, Qani Prespa, Sally Selfo Nexhib, Naqe Myrteza Premtaj, Shaban Semsuddini, and Nancy Topulli of the Albanian Islamic Center and the Albanian Bektashi Teqe communities. For assistance with the present extended version of this project, I would like to thank Father Ndue Gjergji, Imam Shuajb Gërguri, Father Nicholas Liolin, Baba Flamur Shkalla, Mark P. Gjokaj, Shije Orhan Shahin, Gjevalin Gegaj, and Shaban Semsuddini. I especially acknowledge the valuable work of Mark P. Gjokaj with the photographs. I would also like to thank the directors at the four agencies in Michigan who worked with refugees from Kosova. Finally, for introducing me to Albanians, their rich culture and traditions, and opening their doors to me for over thirty years, I owe a special debt of gratitude to Baba Rexheb and his community.

SERIES ACKNOWLEDGMENTS

Discovering the Peoples of Michigan is a series of publications that resulted from the cooperation and effort of many individuals. The people recognized here are not a complete representation, for the list of contributors is too numerous to mention. However, credit must be given to Jeffrey Bonevich, who worked tirelessly with me on contacting people as well as researching and organizing material.

The initial idea for this project came from Mary Erwin, but I must thank Fred Bohm, director of the Michigan State University Press, for seeing the need for this project, for giving it his strong support, and for making publication possible. Also, the tireless efforts of Keith Widder and Elizabeth Demers, senior editors at Michigan State University Press, were vital in bringing DPOM to fruition. Keith put his heart and soul into this series, and his dedication was instrumental in its success.

Otto Feinstein and Germaine Strobel of the Michigan Ethnic Heritage Studies Center patiently and willingly provided names for contributors and constantly gave this project their tireless support.

My late wife, Usha Mehta Helweg, was the initial editor. She meticulously went over manuscripts. Her suggestions and advice were crucial. Initial typing, editing, and formatting were also done by Majda Seuss, Priya Helweg, and Carol Nickolai.

Many of the maps in the series were drawn by Fritz Seegers while the graphics showing ethnic residential patterns in Michigan were done by the Geographical Information Center (GIS) at Western Michigan University under the directorship of David Dickason. Additional maps are by Ellen White.

Russell Magnaghi must also be given special recognition for his willingness to do much more than be a contributor. He provided author contacts as well as information to the series' writers. Other authors and organizations provided comments on other aspects of the work. There are many people that were interviewed by the various authors who will remain anonymous. However, they have enabled the story of their group to be told. Unfortunately, their names are not available, but we are grateful for their cooperation.

Most of all, this work is a tribute to the writers who patiently gave their time to write and share their research findings. Their contributions are noted and appreciated. To them goes most of the gratitude.

ARTHUR W. HELWEG, *Series Co-editor*

Contents

I. Who Are the Albanians? 1

II. Journeys to America and Michigan 7

III. Working Together: Religion and Family .13

IV. Growth of Albanian Churches, Mosque, and Muslim
Monastery in Michigan 20

V. Michigan as Refuge from Political Oppression in Europe 27

VI. Ethnic Survival and Contributions of Albanian Americans 37

APPENDICES

Albanian Food 45

Albanian Language 51

Albanian Music *by Suzanne Camino* 55

NOTES 61

References and Suggested Sources 65

Frontispiece. Albanian national hero Skenderbeg and his wife Donika. Painting by Rexhep Goçi.

I. Who Are the Albanians?

A Proud People from Southeast Europe

The Albanians are one of the oldest peoples in Europe. They have long inhabited the western side of the Balkan Peninsula, and they trace their ancestry to the ancient Illyrians. When the Greeks and later the Slavs entered the Balkan peninsula, they pushed the Albanians into the mountainous regions along the Adriatic, much as the Scots and Welsh were pushed into the mountainous regions of the British Isles. The Albanians have maintained their separate linguistic and social identity despite pressures from their more numerous Slav and Greek neighbors. During the five hundred years that the Ottoman Empire ruled the Balkans, the northern Albanian clans were never fully conquered. Albanians excelled as soldiers, again like the Scots,[1] and were famous throughout the Ottoman Empire for their military skills and their *besa*, or word of honor. Albanians began coming as immigrants to America at the end of the nineteenth century when their lands were still under the Ottomans, although many Albanians came after World War II. During that war, Albania was invaded by Italy and Germany. Jews fleeing Nazis sought refuge in Albania where Albanians hid and protected them. Remarkably, Albania was the only country in Europe that had a larger Jewish population at the end of the war than before (Sarner

Figure 1. The most famous Albanian of recent times: Mother Teresa (1910–1997). Photo by Frances Trix.

1997). Most recently, in the spring of 1999, Albanians drew world attention when they were massively expelled from Kosova by Slobodan Milosevic's Serbian forces, only to return in the summer thanks to NATO actions.

While Albanians as a political force in Europe have generally been overshadowed by their more numerous Balkan neighbors, individual Albanians have achieved renown. The Roman emperor Diocletian was of Albanian descent, as was Pope Clement XI. The Albanian national hero, Gjergj Kastrioti, also known as Skenderbeg, held off Ottoman armies for twenty-four years in the fifteenth century, a feat unmatched by any other European leader. During Ottoman rule, thirty grand vizirs were of Albanian origin as was the greatest of the Ottoman lexicographers.[2] In more recent times, the Albanian novelist Ismail Kadare has been widely translated; but the most prominent Albanian of the twentieth century was Mother Teresa,[3] Nobel Peace Prize winner and founder of the Sisters of Charity.

The history of the Albanians in Europe has been complicated by their location, either between or on the edge of large empires. The road connecting Rome and Byzantium, the Via Ignatia, went through the center of Albanian lands. Reflecting this split, Albanians to the

Figure 2. Where Albanians Live in Southeast Europe.

north became Roman Catholic, while those to the south became Orthodox Christian. After the Ottomans conquered the Balkans in the fifteenth century, many Albanians, particularly in the central regions, converted to Islam. The Ottoman Turks ruled Albanian lands as a western edge of their empire until the twentieth century. Albania's difficult mountainous terrain, reinforced by the Ottoman political and cultural boundary, helps explain why the British historian Edward Gibbon could say of Albania in the eighteenth century that it was "within sight of Italy (across the Adriatic), but less well known than the interior of America."

Albanians began immigrating to America from Southeast Europe at the end of the nineteenth century. They settled principally in New England, the New York area, and the industrial cities of the Midwest. An early result of their immigration was an intensification of national consciousness and organized political action (Federal Writers' Project 1975: VII). In particular, Albanian immigrants in America founded the Albanian Orthodox Church in Boston in 1908 as separate from the Greek Orthodox Church. (At that time Greece and the Greek Orthodox Church actively discouraged Albanian nationalism because of Greek claims to southern Albanian lands.[4]) Albanian immigrants in America also collected funds before and after World War I, and sent representatives to lobby in Washington and Paris for the survival of their homeland. The newly ordained Albanian Orthodox Metropolitan, Fan Noli, had a personal relationship with President Woodrow Wilson that was particularly critical at the peace conferences after the war, since Albania's neighbors (Greece, Yugoslavia, and Italy) all had designs on Albanian territory. President Wilson's support for smaller nations is still remembered among Albanians in America and in the Balkans.

Albanian immigrants first came to Michigan from New England and New York in the second decade of the twentieth century. They included both Orthodox Christian and Muslim Albanians from the villages and towns of the prefectures of Korçë and Gjirokastër in southern Albania. Together they organized an active branch (#33) of *Vatra*, the Pan-Albanian Federation that had been founded in 1912 in Boston to coordinate nationalist support for the survival of Albania in the volatile politics of the Balkans at that time.

Although the Albanian immigrants to Detroit formed a branch of a nationalist Albanian organization early on, they did not immediately form religious organizations. The pressing need for religious leaders in America was for burials. Since Detroit was far from Boston and New York—the places of greatest political sensitivity to European political activity—the Orthodox Christian Albanians in Detroit could still find local Greek Orthodox priests to bury them, while the Albanian Muslims were able to go to the Lebanese Imam Karoub. It was not until 1929 that the Albanian Orthodox in Detroit gathered to organize what became Saint Thomas Orthodox Church. The Albanian Muslims waited until after World War II to organize the Moslem-American Society (1946); they founded the mosque in 1949 and the *teqe* or "monastery" of the Bektashi Order,[5] a Sufi or mystic Muslim Order, in 1954. Twenty years later when Albanian Catholics began arriving in number from northern Albania and Montenegro, two Albanian Catholic churches were also founded in metropolitan Detroit.

Thus, in their gradual organization of ethnic religious institutions, the Detroit community of Albanian immigrants appears to have followed the pattern of many other immigrant groups. Yet, viewed in the framework of other Albanian communities in America, the Detroit Albanian community stands out in several ways. First, the Detroit community had an unusual cohesiveness and unity, one that crossed religious lines and that manifested itself in unusual generosity to national Albanian cultural actions. Second, the Detroit Albanian community appears to have remained more traditional in its orientation than the other large immigrant Albanian communities. For example, in the 1940s when both Albania itself and the Albanian immigrant communities in Boston and New York were affected by European socialist and communist ideologies, Detroit remained staunchly nationalist and unaffected by the new ideologies. Moreover, during the time that Albania, which was taken over by Communists in 1944, became a communist and eventually an atheist state, the Detroit Albanians founded the traditional religious institutions of mosque (1949) and teqe (1954).

When Baba Rexheb, the leader of the Albanian Bektashi Teqe in Michigan, first came to America in 1952, he tried to found a teqe in New York. But there was too much political discord and disarray from the new post-war situation in the Balkans. Instead, an Albanian Communist in New York suggested that he go to Detroit where the Albanian community was more stable. The Bektashi teqe that Baba founded in Michigan became the central Albanian Bektashi teqe in North America, with members across the Albanian diaspora as far away as Belgium, the former Yugoslavia, Turkey, and Australia.

II. Journeys to America and Michigan

Earliest Albanian Immigrants to Michigan

The earliest Albanian immigrants to the United States were Orthodox Christians who came at the end of the nineteenth century from the region of Korçe in southeastern Albania. They emigrated for economic reasons, to escape poverty exacerbated by the political turmoil of nationalist movements in the Balkans. Their plan was to borrow money for ship passage, to find work, to live as cheaply as possible, to accumulate money, and then to return to the Balkans for good. A longtime Albanian Orthodox Christian resident of Detroit, Ted Peppo, noted that his father was a "Columbus," in that he had first come to America from Korçe in 1890. The father arrived in New York, then went to Boston (always the center for Albanian Orthodox Christians). He worked, made some money, traveled back to Albania, and then returned to America with his oldest son. They worked in a hotel in Akron, Ohio, after which the father returned for yet another son. They worked in Ashtabula, Ohio, then in a furniture factory in Jamestown, New York, and finally came to Detroit in 1914. The oldest brother served in the U.S. Army in World War I, and used his bonus to bring the rest of the family to America in 1920. The youngest son, Ted, went to school in Detroit, but with the Depression, began to work in a restaurant. He eventually

owned his own restaurant, and in 1935 traveled back to Korçe in southern Albania with his mother to find a bride.

Traveling back and forth between Albania and the United States
was very common among early Albanian immigrants, as was movement from city to city in the Midwest. Clearly this was a life for men
alone, rather than families. Indeed these men often lived with other
"bachelors" in groups, helping each other out as best they could.
Women were brought over when life became more stable, with the
Albanian Orthodox Christians tending to bring women to America earlier than the Albanian Muslims.

One of the earliest Albanian Muslim immigrants to Michigan was
Orhan Ali of Voskop, a village in the region of Korçe, who arrived in
America in 1905. He traveled back and forth between America and
Albania, only bringing his son to Detroit in 1929. Ten years later, in
1939, his son went back and returned with his mother and a bride.
Orhan Ali was unusual, however, because of his early immigration to
America and because he eventually brought his wife. Many of the early
Muslim Albanian immigrants either never married or never brought
their wives to America. Unlike the Orthodox Christian Albanians, the
Albanian Muslims did not come to America in any significant numbers
until after 1913.

The invasion of southern Albania by Greece in 1913 precipitated the
coming of Albanian Muslims. Prior to that, Albania had been under
Ottoman rule for several hundred years and many Muslim Albanians
had held low-level administrative positions under their fellow Muslim
Ottomans. But with Albania's declaration of independence from the
Ottoman Empire in 1912 and the ensuing invasion by the Greeks, many
Muslim Albanians in southern Albania had lost their means of liveli-
hood. With the Greek invasion came the burning of villages and even
greater economic hardship for an already hard-pressed area.

At the same time, Albanian Orthodox Christians as well as Albanian
Muslims in America were drawn to Detroit to work in the automobile
factories. Once in Detroit some Albanians labored in the factories, but
most preferred jobs where they could become their own boss. Thus they
worked in Coney Islands, in restaurants, in bars, in coffeehouses, and as
barbers and tailors. With the worsening of conditions in southern

Albania, Albanians in Detroit helped relatives and other people from the same town come to Michigan. This first stage of Albanian immigration ended, however, with the imposition of immigrant quota regulations in the 1920s, and with what appeared to be an improvement of conditions in Albania. This hope, however, was short-lived because Albania had neither the resources nor a stable environment for its economy to develop. Before the young country could get its economy in order, Italy invaded in 1939, followed by the Germans in World War II.

Albanian Immigrants after World War II

The second stage of Albanian immigration to the United States and Michigan took place after World War II, from 1945 to 1960. The immigrants of this time differed from the earlier ones in that they came principally for political rather than economic reasons. Many had been allied with anti-Communist resistance groups in Albania such as *Balli Kombëtar* (the National Front) and *Legalitet* (the royalist followers of King Zog). They fled for their lives after the Communists gained power in 1944. They also differed from the earlier immigrants in that they came not just from the towns of southern Albania, but from all regions of the country and all classes of society. The first clerics of both the Michigan mosque and teqe are from this second group of Albanian immigrants.

The third stage of Albanian immigration to America and Michigan occurred from the 1960s through the 1980s. The immigrants of this group took advantage of the lifting of quota regulations, and are principally from Albanian populations outside Albania in what were then the neighboring republics of Yugoslavia.[6] These minority populations are found outside Albania because when the Great Powers first drew Albania's borders in 1913, they left half of all Albanians in the surrounding countries of Greece and Yugoslavia. In particular, these people include Muslim Albanians from the Lake Prespa region of Macedonia and the Kosova region in Serbia, as well as Roman Catholic Albanians from Montenegro and Kosova. They came to the United States for economic reasons—Montenegro, Kosova, and Macedonia were the poorest regions of Yugoslavia—but also for political reasons. As the largest population in Yugoslavia without their own republic, Albanians in Kosova

experienced prejudice and even persecution in the 1950s and 1960s, followed by martial law and wholesale firing from jobs in 1981 and again
in 1990-91. It further appeared that the Montenegrin government
actively encouraged emigration of Albanians from their republic.

Albanian Immigrants after the Fall of Communism in Europe

The 1990s brought yet another change in Albanian immigration as
Albanians from Albania proper, who had been forbidden to travel outside of their country from 1944 to 1991, joined those family members in
America who had arrived decades earlier. The opportunity came as a
result of the Albanian Communist regime's loss of control in 1991 and
official fall from power in 1992. At the same time, conditions in Kosova
went from strict repression and martial law in the late 1980s to open
violence in the spring of 1998. This violence culminated in the massive
expulsion of Albanians from Kosova in the spring of 1999. The United
States welcomed over 10,000 Kosovar refugees in June and July of 1999.
Many of these people came to stay with relatives in Michigan, although
some of these families returned to Kosova within six months.

Problems Documenting Albanian Immigrants in all Periods

When considering the numbers of Albanians who came to America
during these different stages of immigration, it is important to remem-
ber that Albania itself is a relatively small country—about the size of
Holland or Maryland in land area—with a population of some three
million, and another four million Albanians living in the neighboring
regions of Greece, Macedonia, Kosova, and Montenegro. It is also
important to note that for all the periods of Albanian immigration to
America, official figures are of little assistance. In the first period of
immigration, there was no separate country listing for Albanians.
Rather they were recorded as Greeks or Turks or as nationals of the
country from which they sailed. Still, in the late 1930s, the Albanian
population in the United States was estimated to be in the range of
35,000 to 60,000 people, most of whom were Orthodox Christians living in New England (Federal Writers' Project 1975: 5). In the second

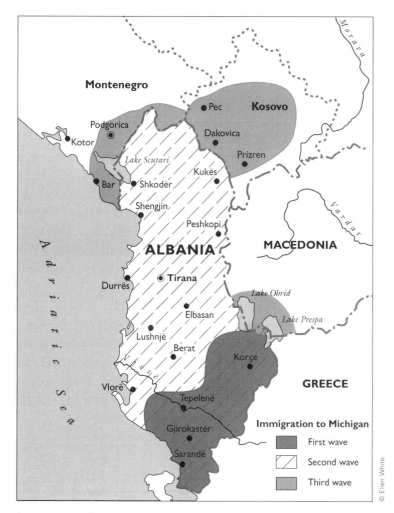

Figure 3. Many Albanians live in countries surrounding Albania.

period of immigration, just after World War II, U.S. Immigration and Naturalization figures list fewer than two hundred Albanians entering the country (Nagi 1989: 5). But in Detroit alone there are many more Albanians who came at this time.

In the third period, from the 1960s to the 1980s, official numbers are not any more useful as most Albanian immigrants came from Yugoslavia and are therefore listed indiscriminately as Yugoslavs. (To further render official numbers meaningless, a number of Roman Catholic Albanians from Montenegro came to Detroit by way of Mexico.) As for the 1990s, Albanian communities in both New York and Detroit have swelled greatly in numbers, but many of the new arrivals have come by way of other countries and again, except for those from Albania proper, their passports identify them not as Albanians, but as former residents of Macedonia or Yugoslavia.

Understandably, then, estimates of Albanian population in the United States in the late twentieth century have a broad range. In 1989 the *Albanian Catholic Bulletin* estimated that there were 250,000 Albanian Americans. This of course did not include those who came in the 1990s. A more recent estimate of Albanian population in the United States is 400,000 in 1998. By 2000, Albanian Americans, including immigrants and their children and their children's children may number more than 500,000, according to the National Albanian American Council (personnel communication, spring, 2000).

In Michigan in 1990, there were an estimated several thousand Orthodox Christian Albanians, more than 10,000 Muslim Albanians, and between 15,000 to 25,000 Roman Catholic Albanians,[7] for a total of some 35,000 religiously affiliated Albanians. In addition, there are Albanians in the Detroit area who are not affiliated with religious institutions and Albanians from Greece whose younger generation has been Hellenized. Some community leaders estimated total Albanian population in Michigan as high as 55,000 in 1991.[8] With added immigration from Albania, Montenegro, Kosova, and Macedonia in the 1990s, along with the movement of Albanians from other parts of North America to Michigan, natural increase and the Kosovar refugees, local leaders estimate that in 2000 there were 70,000 Albanian Americans in Michigan.

III. Working Together: Religion and Family

Albanian Muslims and Christians

It would seem that the division of Albanians among different religious traditions could only weaken them in the face of their more numerous neighbors. But Albanians have generally seen themselves as Albanians first, and as Christian or Muslim second. This was apparent in the Ottoman Empire when Albanian Christian and Muslim leaders met and together formed the League of Prizren (1878), which worked to protect Albanian lands from their neighbors. Indeed, of all the peoples of the Ottoman Empire, the Albanians were the first to cross religious lines for national purposes. In America Albanian immigrants, both Orthodox Christian and Muslim, worked together early on in Vatra, the Pan-Albanian Federation whose founders were the Orthodox Christian Metropolitan, Fan Noli, and the Muslim, Faik Konitza.

In Michigan Orthodox Christian Albanians and Muslim Albanians worked together in Vatra for the survival of their homeland. Albanian Christians and Muslims in Michigan also met regularly for the annual Flag Day (November 28, the day of the declaration of Albanian independence) and for the summer picnic. Those who grew up in the 1930s and 1940s speak of friendships and such regular gatherings with Albanians of the other faith.

As evidence of Christian-Muslim cooperation in the Detroit community, the list of people who contributed money to offset the publication cost of Fan Noli's Albanian translation of the liturgy and prayer book of the Orthodox Church (*Kremtore e Kishes Orthodokse*, 1947) includes names of forty-six Albanian Muslims in Detroit.[9] The commemorative album of Fan Noli's forty years in America (*Albumi Dyzetvjeçar në Amerikë 1906-1946 i Hirësisë tij Peshkop Fan Noli*, 1948) also includes a list of people who donated money for its publication costs, of whom thirty-seven of the fifty-seven from Detroit were Muslim. On a lesser scale, Christian Albanians also donated funds for Muslim Xhevat Kallajxhi's account of Bektashism and the Albanian Teqe in America (*Bektashizmi dhe Teqeja Shqiptare n'Amerikë*, 1964). Muslims donated to the building of the Orthodox church, and Orthodox Christians donated to the Muslim teqe. More recently, a prominent Bektashi Muslim Albanian businessman in Detroit, Ekrem Bardha, gave $1,000 to the building of the new Orthodox church in a western suburb of Detroit in the 1980s. He also donated the cost of flag poles for an Albanian Roman Catholic Church in an eastern suburb of Detroit.

Longtime Albanian residents of Detroit note, however, that while Orthodox Christians and Muslims got along well in earlier times, their relationship became less personal after World War II. This was partly due to the greater number of people in each community. When they were fewer in number during the first half of the twentieth century, their common concern with the fate of their homeland and their common origin in southern Albania had brought them together. But after World War II, each group became more involved within its own community. In addition, people within and across the communities were polarized in their responses to the new Communist regime in Albania. Some did not castigate the new regime for fear of the fate of their relatives still living in Albania, others did not understand it, while others were outwardly against it. This was also the time of the founding of the Muslim religious institutions in Detroit, one of which was led by Baba Rexheb, who had been active in resisting the Communists. Nevertheless Muslims and Christians continued to invite the clerics of the other religions to holiday celebrations in their communities. For example, the priest and the imam would be invited to the Bektashi teqe for the main Bektashi holidays.

Compared to the earlier Orthodox and Muslim Albanian immigrants, the Roman Catholic Albanians, most of whom have come since 1967, have not had as close a relationship with other Albanians. Roman Catholic Albanians differ from the earlier groups of Albanian immigrants in that they are *Gegs,* or northern Albanians, who come largely from Montenegro, Kosova, and northern Albania. They speak a different dialect than the southern Albanians who are known as *Tosks.* Further, the Roman Catholics are new immigrants, whereas the Orthodox and many of the Muslim Albanians have been in America for two generations. Most of the Muslim and non-affiliated Albanians from Kosova who have come in the 1980s and 1990s are also northerners. Nevertheless, at a political gathering of Albanians from all regions and faiths in the mid-1970s, the Bektashi Baba stated that as the Catholics did not yet have a church we should all help them. Indeed both teqe and mosque assisted in the purchase of a church for Albanian Catholics.

Albanian Family Bonds

From a cultural perspective, Albanian Muslims and Christians of all denominations share many basic values and practices. Family bonds are especially strong. Sons and daughters often work long hours in family businesses such as restaurants, dry cleaners, or beauty salons. The sons eventually take over from their fathers and carry on the family enterprise. Several generations of a family often live together in the same house. The society is patriarchal with the father having clear authority. The traditional pattern is that when a man marries, his bride comes to live with her husband's family. This has practical implications for care of the elderly, and care of grandchildren, but also it puts the young bride in a challenging position since she is the new member who often must serve multiple members of her husband's family, in addition to raising her own children.

Albanian American girls often are more restricted in their social life than their brothers. They are expected to marry relatively young by

American standards, usually between eighteen and twenty-two, although this is changing as more Albanian girls go to college. There is strong preference for marriage within the Albanian community, particularly among Muslims and Roman Catholics. There is even an added preference that the families be from the same region, although there is a prohibition among northern Albanians against marrying from the same extended clan as the father. Certainly marriage within the Albanian community helps preserve the language. There is also the practical consideration that older relatives often do not speak English and they will feel more comfortable with a new bride or groom who is accustomed to their ways and who speaks their language.

Second generation Albanian Americans favor having separate homes, but they often live near their parents and siblings. It is not uncommon to find from two to five houses with related families living next to each other. In Michigan, Albanians have not settled whole neighborhoods to the same extent as Italians and Mexicans. Partly this reflects their relative numbers and the relative lateness of their arrival in

Figure 4. Albanian American extended family in Michigan. Photo by Mark P. Gjokaj.

America. But this also relates to the regionalism in the Albanian community in that Albanians from different regions of the Balkans do not often choose to live next to each other. Sometimes people would like to live closer to each other, but homes are not available. In these cases, visiting patterns are more reflective of ties than geographic proximity.

In Michigan, Albanians have largely settled in the Detroit metropolitan area, in Wayne, Oakland, and Macomb counties. The municipalities in which they are found include Dearborn, Detroit, and Hamtramck for the most recent comers. In these communities, coffeehouses, where only men go, serve as centers of Albanian camaraderie.

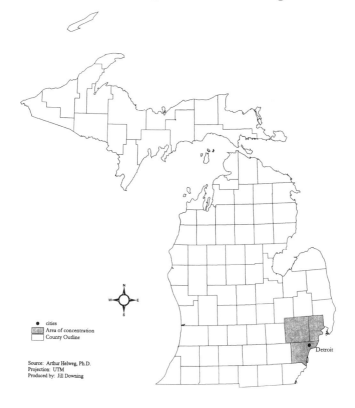

Albanian Population in Michigan

● cities
▨ Area of concentration
☐ County Outline

Source: Arthur Helweg, Ph.D.
Projection: UTM
Produced by: Jill Downing

Figure 5. Counties in Michigan Where Most Albanian Americans Live.

These were even more important in earlier times when many Albanian men did not have families in America. Subsequently, immigrants in these areas have moved to the suburbs of Warren, Sterling Heights, Rochester Hills, Bloomfield Hills, Farmington Hills, Plymouth, Taylor, Westland, and Allen Park. Albanian women have been somewhat more restricted, but thanks to the telephone and visiting customs, news travels fast across the communities.

Engagement parties and weddings are important social events that promote social cohesion. Showers for the bride-to-be are often large and the number of gifts is considerable. The wedding receptions are also large and provide a way for people to stay in touch with one another. People in Albanian communities as far away as Waterbury, Connecticut; New York City; Hackensack, New Jersey; Toronto, Chicago, or even Southeast Europe come to Michigan for weddings of their relatives. Wedding receptions provide a place for young people to meet each other, although it is often older people in the community who are instrumental in suggesting and arranging marriages.

Despite their common language, history, and social practices, there is almost no marriage across the Muslim/Christian divide within the Albanian community in Michigan. Outside the Albanian community there has been some cross-religion marriage. For example, Albanian men who had escaped early from the Communist regime after World War II and who found themselves in camps in Greece sometimes married Greek Christian women because there were so few Albanian women outside Albania. But for Muslim women there are stronger sanctions against marrying non-Muslims. Indeed, some of the best educated and most high achieving Albanian American Muslim women have not married due to the religious prohibition and a lack of similarly educated available Albanian Muslim men, many of whom did marry outside their faith and community. There are some Albanian Muslims and many Albanian Orthodox who grew up in America who have married outside the Albanian community. They have married American Christians and sometimes Jews, or more rarely, Muslims of Arab descent. Yet the first preference among most Albanian families in America is still that their children marry Albanians of the same religious background. However this cultural boundary was not maintained

Figure 6. Albanian American bride and groom at wedding in Michigan. Photo by Mark P. Gjokaj.

in Albania during Communist times (1944-1991). Religion was first denigrated and then outlawed when Albania declared itself an atheist state in 1967. Consequently recent immigrants from Albania have married Albanians whose grandparents were of different religious backgrounds.

IV. Growth of Albanian Churches, Mosque, and Muslim Monastery in Michigan

Among Albanian immigrants in Michigan, the Orthodox Christians were the first to organize a religious institution, followed by the Muslims, and most recently the Roman Catholics. The saga of their institutions reflects the growth of their financial base as well as movement of people from Detroit to the suburbs.

The Albanian Society of Orthodox Christians founded the St. Thomas community in a private home in 1929, but because of the Depression, their plans were put on hold. They bought their first church in downtown Detroit in 1943, then built a new church on the west side of the city in 1956. They decided in 1978 to seek a new location, this time in Farmington Hills, a northern suburb of Detroit. They broke ground in 1980, and paid off all debts on the land by 1988.[10]

The Albanian American Moslem Society was founded in Detroit in 1945. Unlike the Orthodox group, its Society came to include Albanian Muslims from Ohio, western New York, and eastern Pennsylvania. By 1949, at the time of its Second Congress, the society had secured an Albanian imam or Muslim religious leader who had studied in Egypt, Imam Vehbi Ismail from Shkodër in northern Albania. At this Congress, the guests of honor included the governor of the state of Michigan, the mayor of the city of Detroit, the president of the Detroit City Council, and the state chairman of the Democratic Committee.[11] Then, in 1950, the Muslims rented and subsequently purchased a former church on the west side of Detroit for the first Albanian mosque in America.[12] In 1964 they built their own mosque in Harper Woods, a suburb on the east side of Detroit. At the "Sunday School" conducted by the mosque, Albanian American children learned about their religion and also how to read and write Albanian.

The Albanian Islamic Center in Michigan has grown with new arrivals from Kosova in the 1980s and the 1990s. They even have a second imam, Imam Shuajb Gërguri, from Prishtina in Kosova, who came to Michigan in 1996 to work with the original imam at the Islamic Center.

Figure 7. Albanian Islamic Center in Harper Woods, Michigan. Photo by Frances Trix.

The other Albanian Muslim institution, the Bektashi Teqe, also drew on members of the Albanian American Moslem Society and grew around the coming of a Bektashi cleric to Detroit in 1953, Dervish Rexheb. Bektashi teqes are traditionally located in quiet but accessible areas. A farm with eighteen acres of land, southwest of Detroit, was purchased, and in 1954 Baba[13] Rexheb opened the first Albanian American Teqe Bektashiane. For the first twenty years the teqe supported itself by growing soybeans, corn, and vegetables, and by selling eggs. But as its staff aged they were not so active in the fields, the community built apartments alongside the teqe to provide monthly support for the "Muslim monastery"

Early relations between the mosque and teqe were not without difficulties. Some members of the mosque feared that a second Albanian Muslim institution would divide the Albanian Muslims living in Michigan. Others feared that by supporting a teqe for Baba Rexheb, a man who had opposed the Communists in Albania, they would be endangering their own relatives in then-Communist Albania. Finally, there were theological differences between the mosque, which follows orthodox Sunni Islam, and the teqe which draws as well from more eastern mystic traditions.

A teqe, however, is never meant to serve as a substitute for a mosque; rather, it has a complementary function, offering people a more personal and mystical venue to their faith.[14] And so in Michigan, as earlier in Albania and Turkey, the mosque and teqe developed a working cooperative relationship. In particular, the mosque holds daily prayers, the weekly Friday prayers, the special prayers for Ramadan, and celebrates the two main Sunni Muslim holidays (*Eid al-Fitr* and *Eid al-Adha*). The imam performs most marriages and funerals. In turn, the teqe celebrates two other additional holidays (*Nevruz* and *Ashure*) and holds the ten-day fast of *Matem*. It further conducts the private rituals for initiated members as well as sessions of *muhabbet* for praise of God. The teqe also serves as a retreat where people may come and stay for various lengths of time. Bektashis, other Muslims, and some Christians request special prayers from the Baba for all manner of personal concerns, ranging from health and good fortune in work to new homes and the birth of children (Trix 1997).

Figure 8. Baba Rexheb was the religious head of the First Albanian-American Bektashi Teqe in Taylor, Michigan, from its founding in 1954 to his passing in 1995. Photo by Asllan Halim.

Among the Muslim immigrants since 1960 are people from the Lake Prespa region of Macedonia. Some of them are most loyal to the teqe, and together with other Muslim Albanians, have supported the construction of both the *turbe,* the mausoleum for Baba Rexheb on teqe grounds and a large addition to the teqe consisting of guest rooms, a meeting room, and a new kitchen, completed in 1991. Baba Rexheb passed from this world in August, 1995. The Bektashi Teqe is now led by Baba Flamur Shkalla, who came to Michigan in 1995 from the region of Durrës, Albania.

As for recent Christian Albanian immigrants to Michigan, they are largely Roman Catholics from Montenegro, Kosova, and northern Albania. They are a tight community, largely made up of people from Gruda, Hoti, Triepsh, and other clans in the region of Malësia e Madhe in northern Albania and Montenegro.

A key person in Catholic Albanian immigration to Detroit was Prenk Gruda. He was born in the Albanian region of Montenegro in 1912; he was educated and employed as a history teacher in Albania. In 1951, he escaped from Albania to Yugoslavia. Two years later he again escaped, this time to Austria. He made his way to the United States and then to Detroit, where he was sponsored by a fellow Catholic Albanian.[15] In 1967, Tito declared an amnesty and Prenk Gruda returned to visit his mother in Yugoslavia, where he saw again the discrimination against Albanians. He convinced many Albanians to travel to refugee camps in Italy, set up by the Roman Catholic Church. From there he helped sponsor a remarkable number of these families as immigrants to Detroit.[16]

Many Roman Catholic Albanians in the late 1960s and 1970s followed this route to Michigan. The founding priest of Our Lady of the Albanians, Father Primus Prenk Ndrevashaj, who himself escaped from Albania in 1952, served on the staff of the Pontifical Office of Immigration in Rome, through which thousands of Catholic Albanians made their way to the United States, principally to New York and Detroit.

Figure 9. Flag Day at St. Paul's Roman Catholic Church, one of two Albanian Roman Catholic congregations in Michigan. The young children are in traditional Albanian garb. Patriotism, loyalty and gratitude to the United States have long been common themes among immigrant communities. Photo by Mark P. Gjokaj.

Figure 10. Albanians at the train station in Prishtina, 1 April 1999, during expulsions from Kosova. The photo is by Vuk Brankovic, and the permission gratefully accorded by Agence France-Presse.

In Detroit the Albanian Roman Catholic community was officially founded in 1972. After renting several churches in Detroit, the congregation split into two groups. One group purchased a former Lutheran church in Beverly Hills, a northern suburb of Detroit in 1976. This became Our Lady of the Albanians, and a rectory was added to the property. This church, which was first led by Father Prenk Ndrevashaj is now led by Father Ndue Gjergji. Father Ndue Gjergji came to Michigan in 1997 from Stublla near Gjilan in Kosova. The other group of Albanian Catholics, under Don Prenk Camaj from Montenegro, bought land in Warren, a suburb on the east side of Detroit, where they built St. Paul's Albanian Catholic Church in 1976. It is now a large congregation with many weekly social and cultural activities. Its current leader, Father Anton Kçira, came to Michigan in 1989 from Gjakova in Kosova. Indeed the congregation, under Father Anton Kçira, has grown so rapidly that they have purchased property further to the north in Rochester Hills where they are building a church and hope to move in 2002.

V. Michigan as Refuge from Political Oppression in Europe

In the 1990s, new Albanian immigrants to Michigan came principally from Albania and Kosova where they had experienced political oppression. Those from Albania had lived under one of the strictest Communist regimes, a Stalinist dictatorship that had restricted and controlled most aspects of its peoples' lives. As for those from Kosova, earlier they had been economically better off than those in Albania, but in the 1990s they had experienced a growing loss of civil liberties and a growing increase in police violence (Human Rights Watch 1994) under the policies of Serbian leader Slobodan Milosevic. When they came to Michigan their accounts of what was going on in Kosova contributed to the politicization of Albanian Americans, who organized to better lobby for support of their ethnic kin in Yugoslavia.

Looking first at those new immigrants from Albania, they had experienced not only political oppression but also isolation for over forty years from the rest of the world. It was only after the fall of the Berlin Wall in 1989, when communism was no longer a viable political ideology in the rest of Eastern Europe, that Albania's isolation lessened. In 1991, crowds in Albania demonstrated against their Communist government and destroyed large statues of Enver Hoxha, the long-lasting dictator, and other monuments to the Communist Party that had ruled

Albania since 1944. In pent up anger, the crowds also destroyed many state enterprises where they had been forced to work for scant wages. Albanians voted the Communist Party out of power in the election of 1992. The extent to which Albania was underdeveloped and lacking in economic and political infrastructure then became clear.

The immigrants from Albania in the 1990s were not escaping direct political oppression but rather the instability that had been left in its wake. Nevertheless they had been affected by Hoxha's regime in several ways. Unlike earlier Albanian immigrants, the new immigrants tended not to be closely affiliated with any religious institution when they first arrived, although some subsequently became practicing Catholics and Muslims. This is not surprising since religion had been illegal in Albania since 1967. Rather, they brought an identity based more on Albanian literature, music, and song—areas that the Communist Party had allowed and encouraged. Many excellent Albanian teachers, singers, and musicians came to Michigan during the 1990s. In recognition of educational needs of Albanians, St. Mary's College in Orchard Lake, Michigan, started a program for Albanian students. Teachers like Agron Fico, a folklorist from Albania who emigrated in the 1990s, taught in the program. Media professional Thoma Gellçi and his wife Diana founded a newspaper, *Albanian House*. Many came seeking technical and professional educational opportunities and enrolled in programs at Wayne State University in Detroit. Yet, before they could pursue education, many had the hardship of paying off loans they had incurred for the cost of passage for the members of their families. In addition, their experience under a severe Communist regime left them without the political orientation and the organizational skills that had so characterized of Albanians from earlier times.

In contrast, the new Albanian immigrants from Kosova in the 1990s had significant political and organizational skills, developed out of necessity in their difficult situation in Yugoslavia. To understand their situation in the 1990s and their expulsion from Kosova in 1999, it is important to consider earlier conditions in Yugoslavia. In the 1980s, communism declined as a viable political ideology in Yugoslavia. In its place strong nationalistic sentiments took hold among the Serbs, the Croats, and to a lesser extent, among the Kosovar Albanians. And while

Serbs were a distinct majority in the country of Yugoslavia, they were an ever-declining minority in the province of Kosova. Serbs and Monte-negrins, who had been privileged in Kosova and who had constituted twenty-one percent of the population of Kosova in 1971, had begun migrating out of Kosova in the 1970s because of unemployment, lack of good housing, and for better economic opportunities elsewhere in Yugoslavia and Western Europe (Vickers 1998:195). In the 1980s they continued to leave Kosova for the same reasons but also for fear of the ever growing Albanian population and from alleged abuses by individ-ual Albanians. Apart from the political issues, Kosovar Albanians had one of the highest birth rates in Europe, while the Serbs had a much lower rate. As Serbian nationalism grew in Yugoslavia, it took the minor-ity situation of Serbs in Kosova as an issue to rally around. Indeed, Slobodan Milosevic came to power by calling attention to the Serb minority in Kosova. To bolster the position of the Serbs in Kosova and to decrease political power of Albanians there, Milosevic abrogated Kosova's autonomous province status in 1989, thereby returning it to direct control by Belgrade.

The decade from 1989 to 1999 was a time of growing oppression for Kosovar Albanians, one that began with great civic displacement and ended with massive expulsions. In the spring of 1990, the government in Belgrade dismissed all Kosovar Albanian police; in the summer of 1990, it fired all Albanian media professionals in Kosova. In the fall of 1990, the government in Belgrade purged Albanians from the Kosova Parliament and dismissed Albanian doctors and health workers. Also in 1990, the government in Belgrade dismissed all Albanians from other state positions and hired Serbs or Montenegrins to fill all municipal jobs. The next year, in 1991, the government in Belgrade fired all Albanian staff at the University of Prishtina. At the same time it expelled all 27,000 Albanian students from the University, leaving only Serb fac-ulty and students at the university. As for Albanian students in high school and elementary school, the government in Belgrade first sus-pended the salaries of all Albanian teachers, while at the same time it more than doubled the salaries of Serbian and Montenegrin teachers. It then all laid off all Albanian teachers in August of 1991 and forbade Albanian students entry to their former schools. It thereby instituted a powerful form of apartheid, for the more the government in Belgrade took from the Albanians in Kosova, the more it gave to the Serbs there, who by then constituted only 10% of the population. Compounding this, the judicial system had been co-opted and there were frequent police assaults and raids on homes (Mead 1998), arrests, and long prison sentences.

Serbian authorities used these practices to make daily life intolerable for Albanians so that they would leave Kosova. Belgrade's plan was to force Albanians out, and then to colonize Kosova with Serbs. It is estimated that there was 85% unemployment among Albanians in what had already been the poorest region of Yugoslavia. Moreover, violence continued against the civilian Albanian population (Human Rights Watch 1994, 1998). However, the international press paid little attention to these events because it was taken up with the greater conflagration in nearby Bosnia.

The war in Bosnia had begun in 1992 when multiethnic Bosnia (made up of Muslim Bosnians, Croat Bosnians, and Serb Bosnians) declared independence from Yugoslavia. Slobodan Milosevic's government in Belgrade fought to prevent Bosnia's departure from Yugoslavia. The result was a polarizing of groups within Bosnia and a three-year civil war. During this time a large group of Serbs living in the Krahina region of Croatia took advantage of the war in neighboring Bosnia to declare their independence from Croatia. However the Bosnian war resulted in 200,000 people killed and 2 million people displaced, including the surviving Serbs from the Krahina who fled to Serbia. Once in Serbia, many of them were bussed to Kosova to live in the now empty Albanian schools. They were to colonize Kosova when the Albanians left.

It is remarkable that during this time of persecution, Albanians set up their own covert institutions. When the Serbs closed down the main Albanian newspapers, new independent Albanian papers sprang up (Trix 2000a). By the spring of 1992 Albanians had set up a parallel system of schools whose classes met in private homes, a system that operated until 1998. Classes had to move from home to home to avoid police notice. Teachers were paid through the Albanian created government whose funds came from Albanians in Kosova (80%) and in the diaspora

(20%), including those in Michigan, who taxed themselves at 3% of their income. The funds in the diaspora were funneled through main banks in New York and Switzerland to the LDK (Democratic League of Kosova), the main Albanian political party of Kosova, which turned them over to the Albanian created government for dispersal. This was the first time that Albanians contributed systematically to the financial assistance of other Albanians who were not their relatives. Albanians elected their own Parliament, outside the capital city of Prishtina, and Ibrahim Rugova, literary scholar and president of the Writers' Union, as their president.

Rugova and the party he led, the LDK, put forth a policy of non-violence and civic-mindedness. Kosovar refugees in Michigan later noted that Rugova had brought them hope. He told them that when the Bosnian war was settled, the world would look to their suffering and they would work toward their own state. (It should be added that the Albanians are not the only people who have suffered under the regime of Milosevic. Bosnians and Croats have also suffered, as have fellow Serbs. Indeed many Serbs have left Serbia since Milosevic's rise to power in 1987.) Unfortunately, when the Dayton Accords were signed in 1995, which ended the war in Bosnia, Kosova was not even mentioned.

By 1995, Kosovar Albanians viewed Rugova's policy of non-violence as ineffective and gradually resorted to armed resistance. Yet, the evolving Kosovar Liberation Army (KLA) did not gain popular support until after the killing by Serb forces of fifty-one members of the Jashari family in Drenica in central Kosova in the winter of 1998. Throughout 1998, Serbian paramilitary groups operated with Serbian police and the Yugoslav military to counter the KLA. The result was a terrorization of the populace—largely Albanian but also Serbian; the destruction of Albanian homes, villages, and food sources; and the kidnapping and killing of Albanians and Serbs. By September of 1998, there were an estimated 300,000 internal refugees in Kosova (Mertus 1999:208). Despite the peace talks in October of 1998, and the Rambouillet talks in early 1999, there was a substantial buildup of Serbian military in Kosova. When the NATO air campaign began in late March, 1999, Milosevic implemented *Operation Horseshoe*, designed to expel large numbers of Albanians from Kosova. During the eleven weeks of expulsions, 500

Albanian villages were burned, many women raped, an estimated
10,000 Albanians killed (Cohen & Korn 1999:11), and 850,000 Albanians
sought refuge outside Kosova.

In Michigan during these eleven weeks, Albanians held rallies to
educate people about the situation and to collect funds and supplies
for the refugees. The Albanian American Student Association of Wayne
State University held a political rally in front of the Federal Building in
Detroit the first week of the air campaign. It was well organized and
there were three different flags flown throughout the crowd: American
flags, the most numerous; Albanian flags, the distinctive red and black
flag with the double-headed eagle; and the flag of NATO. During this
week St. Paul's Albanian Catholic Church collected $100,000 for
refugees. Our Lady of the Albanians collected $60,000 for refugees dur-
ing the main period of expulsions. Other Albanian religious centers—
the Mosque, the Teqe, and the Orthodox Church[17]—also collected
thousands of dollars to help the refugees.

As for the refugees themselves, initially the plan was to keep them
close to Kosova in neighboring countries. However Macedonia soon
closed its border to Kosovars, fearing that they would change the
demography of Macedonia. Macedonia only agreed to reopen the border if NATO states immediately accepted refugees. The United States
agreed to take up to 20,000 and, through Operation Provide Rescue,
established a major processing center at the Fort Dix Army base in New
Jersey. In preparation, across America agencies geared up to accept the
refugees. Kosovar Albanian American families initiated sponsorship for
their relatives through these agencies.

In Michigan the federally designated agencies were the Catholic
Archdiocese of Detroit, Episcopal Refugee Relief of St. Paul's Cathedral
in Detroit, Jewish Family Services of Southfield, and Lutheran Immigrant and Refugee Services of the Lutheran Church, also of Detroit.
Refugees in Macedonia whose relatives in America had promised sponsorship were among the first airlifted to America. For those whose des-
tination was Michigan, many came directly from New York. Only a few
families were first processed through Fort Dix.

The above agencies facilitated the sponsorship of Kosovar refugees.
They helped them enroll for English instruction, register for appropriate

social welfare programs, and find jobs. Many organizations in Michigan offered support for the refugees. Some provided a warehouse in Detroit where people could get furniture. Church groups collected clothing, health supplies, and foodstuffs. The Catholic Archdiocese and the Episcopal Cathedral sponsored refugees who had no other sponsors. Their churches took on co-sponsorship of Kosovar refugee families. These churches recognized that the Albanian families who sponsored the refugees were themselves recent immigrants. It was difficult, for example, when a family of fourteen refugees came to live in the house of their relatives who numbered only four. Co-sponsoring churches found housing whose rent they would guarantee for a certain period. Co-sponsoring churches often had members who facilitated entry to educational programs and contact with potential employers. But the lion's share of the resettlement work was handled by relatives and the four agencies. Jewish Family Services had settled many Russian Jews, which prepared them for work with Kosovar refugees. The Lutherans had distinguished themselves with the earlier Bosnian refugees. The Catholic Archdiocese of Detroit brought in the highest number of refugees. And a staff member of the Episcopal effort took on sponsorship of a group of over twenty Kosovars that came through Fort Dix and settled in Hamtramck, Michigan.

Almost all the Kosovar refugees who came to Michigan were Muslims. The agencies designated and funded by the federal government to assist refugees were Christian and Jewish. The co-sponsoring Christian churches were Episcopalian, Presbyterian, Lutheran, Roman Catholic, and Methodist. Jewish, Catholic, Protestant, and Muslim individuals also helped different refugee families. This led to a new sensitivity for Muslims by Christians, which resulted in new ties between Christians and Muslims. One memorable example of this was recounted to me by Sandi Rosso of the Catholic Archdiocese of Detroit.

Apparently an Albanian couple had met at Fort Dix in May of 1999, during the time they were waiting to be resettled in America. They had become engaged and when they came to Detroit through the Catholic Archdiocese of Detroit, they wanted to be married. Some refugees felt it was not appropriate at this time of crisis to have a wedding, but others

Figure 11. Albanian saint, by Rexhep Goçi, courtesy of St. Andrew's Episcopal Church, Ann Arbor, Michigan.

believed that life needed to go on. In any case, Ms. Rosso found herself going to second-hand stores in search of a wedding gown. Since the bride came from a conservative family in Kosova, her gown needed to be conservative as well. The week of the wedding Ms. Rosso finally found an appropriate gown and the couple was married at the Albanian Islamic Center in Harper Woods, just outside Detroit. People from the Catholic Archdiocese of Detroit and the Albanian Islamic Center worked together when planning this wedding and thereby came to appreciate each other. On Albanian Independence Day, 28 November 1999, the Albanian Islamic Center held its usual large gathering and invited staff from the Catholic Archdiocese of Detroit to attend. The Islamic Center presented a certificate to the Catholic Archdiocese of Detroit to acknowledge their work in assisting Albanian refugees.

Another example of cross-cultural understanding spurred by the relationship of Michigan churches with Kosovar refugee families is the Goçi family. The father, Rexhep Goçi, is a well respected painter, teacher, and art historian from Kosova. When he first arrived with his family in Westland, Michigan, in June 1999, one of the ways he responded to the trauma of expulsion was by painting a series of memorable canvasses of Albanian legend and landscape, relating to his homeland. There have been public showings of his work in Ann Arbor. Mr. Goçi presented one painting to American diplomat, Ambassador Walker, who as head of the Kosovo Commission of the Organization for Security and Cooperation in Europe in the winter of 1999, played a crucial role in letting the world know the seriousness of the situation in Kosova. Mr. Goçi presented two other paintings to St. Andrew's Episcopal Church in Ann Arbor in recognition of their generosity after the Kosova crisis.

VI. Ethnic Survival and Contributions of Albanian Americans

A common thread for all Albanian Americans in Michigan—Orthodox, Muslim, Roman Catholic and unaffiliated—has been concern for relatives back in the Balkans. America has been a land of such bounty and stability in comparison to their homelands that they feel bound to help in different ways. For Orthodox Christian Albanians, this concern has taken the shape of providing medicines and foodstuffs for multiple families of relatives, and in the 1990s, helping fund schools in Albania and assisting the education of younger Albanians in America. For Muslim Albanians, concern for relatives in the Balkans has meant sending parcels of food and clothing, lobbying for political support of Albanians in Europe, sponsoring relatives in America, and assisting with adjustment to life in America. For Roman Catholic Albanians, this concern for relatives has included funding village improvements—electricity, roads, churches, and cultural centers, along with the sending of parcels, financial aid, and assistance in immigration and adjustment to life in America. The generous contributions to relatives in Southeast Europe have often meant sacrifices for people who themselves are working to adapt to American life.

The greatest variation among Albanian Americans in Michigan is the degree and rate of acculturation to American life, with the Orthodox

Christians being the most acculturated. This is not surprising as the Orthodox came to America first, and have had the least ongoing immigration of any of the three groups. Education has been an extremely high priority, and children of Albanian Orthodox immigrants include attorneys, engineers, medical doctors, teachers, and corporate executives. In turn, their children are successful in graduate and professional university programs. This success is a contribution to the Detroit-area economy and services.

But with rapid changes, there have been costs in ethnic continuity. The lack of ongoing Orthodox immigration has made it more difficult to marry within the community, and there has been much intermarriage with non-Albanians. Few of the third generation speak Albanian. This is reflected in the liturgy at Saint Thomas, where the current priest, Father Nicholas Liolin, noted that when he first came from the Albanian American community in New York City, thirty years ago, the liturgy was mostly in Albanian, while now it is mostly in English.

A new direction in the Orthodox community appears to be an emphasis on being Orthodox along with being Albanian. The Albanian Orthodox are members of the Orthodox Church in America under Theodosius, Archbishop of Washington and Metropolitan of all America and Canada. In the past thirty years, however, this affiliation at the national level has also included local participation in Detroit in the pan-Orthodox Council (Rumanian, Russian, Serbian, Greek, Bulgarian, Macedonian, Syrian Antiochian) and well as in a regional council of laymen and clergy. In 1950 the Greek Orthodox Church tried to get the Albanian Orthodox to rejoin it. One church in Boston and another in Chicago did so, but St. Thomas refused, making it the western-most Albanian Orthodox church in America.

Muslim Albanians have immigrated to Michigan throughout this century and, as would be expected, those who came earliest are most acculturated to American life. But in contrast to the Orthodox, the Muslims have been more conservative in their traditions and less likely to marry non-Albanians, which was made somewhat easier because of the continual in-migration of Albanian Muslims. Thus, there is more retention of the Albanian language among children born in America, and services at the mosque and the teqe are still largely conducted in

Albanian. Some families even sent children to the University of Prishtina in Kosova in the 1970s and 1980s. Unlike the Orthodox however, Albanian Muslims in Michigan have affiliated more with Albanian Muslims across North America than with other Muslims of different ethnic backgrounds in Michigan. Indeed, Imam Vehbi of the Albanian Islamic Center of Michigan founded and continues to lead an organization, the Presidency of the Albanian Muslim Community in the United States and Canada, to foster unity among Albanian Muslims. In 2000 this organization included fourteen Albanian Islamic Centers in New York, Connecticut, New Jersey, Pennsylvania, Illinois, Florida, Wisconsin, Texas, and Canada. But like the Orthodox Christian Albanians, the Muslim Albanians have also valued education, and there are teachers, engineers, medical doctors, and other professionals among them. For the most part, though, Muslim Albanians have prospered more as entrepreneurs and businessmen, as owners of businesses, including restaurants, Coney Islands, McDonalds, bars, dry cleaners, travel agencies, and newspapers.

Finally, the Roman Catholic Albanians, as new immigrants, found themselves working in restaurants and factories, but there are also business owners among them. Some of the children of these immigrants have become health and legal professionals, as well as teachers and computer specialists. Marriage is largely within the community, and church services are conducted in Albanian. These Albanians are closest to their Balkan roots, and include cultural leaders active in media and the arts. In particular, Roman Catholic Albanians in Michigan supported two regular radio programs in Albanian, and for a time, a special cultural center in Hamtramck. Indeed, one contribution of these recent Albanian immigrants has been the revitalization of areas of Hamtramck, a city within the city of Detroit. They have bought and remodeled storefronts and established businesses and houses where families now reside.

An event in the 1980s that drew Albanians in Michigan together was the imprisonment of Pjetër Ivezaj, a Catholic Albanian teacher and naturalized American, who went from Detroit to Yugoslavia for a visit. When he reached Yugoslavia, authorities there promptly put him in prison for a seven-year sentence. They charged that he had been observed by an UDBA (Yugoslav secret police) agent attending a rally in America against the Yugoslav policy toward Albanians. Both Christian and Muslim Albanians in Michigan rallied and worked through Michigan Republican Congressman William Broomfield to threaten Yugoslavia with loss of most favored nation status if it did not release the American Albanian. This political pressure worked and Ivezaj was set free.

In the early 1990s, humanitarian concern for Albanians in southeast Europe drew Albanians in Michigan together. At that time, Albanians in Albania suffered economic deprivation, those in Kosova suffered political and economic oppression, while Albanians in Macedonia and Montenegro constituted minority populations in unstable states. The Albanian Aid Society was founded in 1991 by Gjavalin Gegaj, a restaurant owner in Oakland County, Michigan, with the express purpose of aiding Albanians in Albania, Kosova, Macedonia, and Montenegro. The Albanian Aid Society drew three representatives from each of the Albanian religious institutions in Michigan (the mosque, the teqe, and the three churches) and thereby was able to tap these institutions for funds for specific projects. It also worked in concert with international aid organizations like Midwest Humanitarian Organization, Mercy Corps International, International Aid (Grand Rapids, Michigan), and the Mother Teresa Charity in Kosova. Its projects have been designated for Albania (1992, 1993), for refugees in Macedonia (1999), and for Kosova (1994, 1996, 1998, 1999, 2000). These projects have included sending clothing and blankets, forty tons of glass for school windows in Albania, medicine and medical equipment, and funding for a maternity wing of a clinic in Kosova. Another organization, St. Anthony's Bread, an Albanian Roman Catholic organization that has fed the hungry for a century, has recently focused on northern Albania. The secretary of the Michigan chapter of St. Anthony's Bread, Mark P. Gjokaj, noted that this intensified with the declining economy in Albania and the entry of thousands of Kosovar refugees in that region.

Besides humanitarian concerns, the pressing political situation of Albanians in Southeast Europe in the mid-1990s also drew Albanian Americans in Michigan to action at the national level. In particular, the

Dayton Accords, which were signed in 1995 to end the war in Bosnia, did not mention the ongoing Serbian oppression of Albanians in Kosova. This neglect of Kosova by the signers of the Dayton Accords undermined the Kosovars' policy of nonviolence. Dr. Sami Repishti of New York founded the National Albanian American Council (NAAC) in 1996 to represent the interests and concerns of Albanian Americans and to foster a better understanding of Albanian issues in the United States.[18] Ekrem Bardha, an Albanian American businessman and community leader from Bloomfield Hills, Michigan, was one of the main founding members of the National Albanian American Council. NAAC is located in Washington DC where it can influence foreign policy makers. On its staff is Albanian American Aferdita Rakipi, the Communications Director of NAAC, who grew up in Dearborn, Michigan. The continual participation of Michigan Albanian Americans in the founding, staffing, and sponsoring of such organizations shows the broad national and international perspective that was so crucial in the political survival of Albanians in the nineteenth and twentieth centuries.

In line with this national and international perspective, Ekrem Bardha is also the current publisher of *Illyria*, the main Albanian American newspaper, published in the Bronx, New York, and founded by Hajdar Bajraktari in 1991. In terms of numbers of people, the Albanian American community in metropolitan New York City is much larger than that of Michigan. But Bardha's leadership of *Illyria* since 1998 and his role at the national level with the NAAC demonstrate the importance of the Michigan community within the larger national Albanian American community.

Julie Black, an attorney and a third generation Albanian American from Waterford, Michigan, is the current president of the Albanian American National Organization (AANO). AANO was founded in 1946 to encourage friendship and unity among all Albanian Americans, to celebrate and thereby perpetuate Albanian customs and traditions, and to support educational pursuits of Albanian Americans through scholarships. In America, where social pressures to assimilate to fit into the general culture are so strong, preservation of one's ethnic heritage takes special effort, which the AANO works to facilitate. Its annual conventions are held in different places, principally in the Northeast and

Midwest where most Albanian Americans reside. It provides a forum where young Albanian Americans can meet. Its annual convention in August, 2000, was in Detroit. Young Albanian Americans from Michigan are thus assuming leadership roles in national organizations. The success in educational attainment and careers—attorneys, pharmacists, physicians, business people, teachers, journalists—represented by the young Albanian Americans at the AANO conventions is indicative of the contribution that Albanian Americans have made to America in general. In the popular culture, the late comedian John Belushi and his actor brother Jim are Albanian Americans who are more widely known.

Since the United States is such a large country, the contributions of Albanian Americans continue to be more apparent in the context of their much smaller homelands. For example there is ongoing concern in the Michigan Albanian American community for the economic conditions in Albania, where the isolationist regime of Enver Hoxha's Communist party (1944-1991) left the country lacking in basic infrastructure. To make matters worse, there were widespread pyramid scams, exposed in 1996, that upset Albania's fragile economy by robbing people of their hard-earned savings. In the face of these dire conditions, as in earlier decades of the twentieth century, Albanian Americans have responded materially and politically, by sending aid to relatives and ethnic kin, and by offering political support for international attention and good government.

Besides material and political contributions, Michigan Albanian Americans have also contributed to their homelands' cultural and spiritual realms. By remaining more traditional than other Albanian communities in America, the Michigan Albanians Americans have preserved religious traditions from their native lands that otherwise could have been lost, especially those of the Bektashi Teqe but also of the mosque and churches. In late 1990, religious services were again held in Albania, thus reversing the policy of state atheism declared in 1967. In the spring of 1991, the Christian Easters of Orthodox and Roman Catholics, the Muslim Ramadan, and the Bektashi Nevruz holidays were again publicly celebrated in Albania after many years of being proscribed. These religious communities looked to Albanian religious communities in America, and especially in the Detroit area, for support in the initial time of reopening and rebuilding. At an International Congress of Bektashis in 1993, in recognition of his leadership, Baba Rexheb of the Michigan Bektashi teqe was elected honorary head of all Bektashis in the world.

Albanians have not only worked together across divisions of Muslim and Christian. Their profound notions of hospitality and the sacredness of the guest extended to Jews who sought and received safe refuge in Albania during World War II. More recently, when over 800,000 Albanians were expelled from Kosova in the spring of 1999, Albanian families in Albania hosted more than half (260,000) of the 460,000 refugees that entered their small country. Albanian families in Macedonia hosted close to half (138,000) of the 300,000 refugees who fled across that border (Trix 2000b). And Albanian families and churches in Montenegro hosted 60,000 refugees. There were international refugee camps set up in Albania and Macedonia, but it was individual Albanian families who hosted most of the refugees, without ever receiving any of the international relief supplies sent to the region. It is no wonder that Albanian Americans were most grateful for the American participation in the NATO air campaign and American agency and church support of Kosovar refugees in the United States. In a world in which religious differences appear to serve as justification for violence, the history of Albanian Muslims and Christians working together, and their ongoing practice and appreciation of hospitality for all people are badly needed models for our times. In this broader framework, contributions of Albanian Americans in Michigan go well beyond Michigan's borders.

APPENDIX 1

Albanian Food*

With the high respect for hospitality and the importance of visiting in Albanian culture, it is no surprise that food preparation and sharing of meals are central to Albanian family life. Non-Albanians who are invited to Albanian American homes often remark on the graciousness with which they are served, and the tastiness of the food. Albanian cuisine is similar to other eastern Mediterranean cuisines. Many Albanian foods, like pilav or yogurt, or stuffed grape leaves or baklava, are common to Greece, Macedonia, and Turkey as well.

Although there are several famous male Albanian restaurateurs in America, like Anthony Athanas, head of Anthony's Pier Four in Boston, or Bruno Selimaj of Bruno's in Manhattan, it is largely the women and girls who do the cooking in the family. Shije Orhan Shahin, an Albanian American who grew up in Grosse Pointe Park, Michigan, recalled when her Albanian grandmother first taught her to cook:

When I was seven years old, my grandmother, Nene (who could roll the thin fillo dough out by hand) took me to the basement kitchen to teach

---

*Note that with some modifications, the recipes in this section are taken from the Albanian cookbook: *Albanian Cookbook,* by the Women's Guild of St. Mary's Albanian Orthodox Church of Worcester, Massachusetts, published in 1977.

me how to make *lakror* (see below). But before we began, she took my little hands in her hands and she dipped my fingertips first in flour and then in sugar and said a short prayer so that I would grow up to be a good cook. I've recalled that day many times in my life.

Lakror is a light dinner pie filled with cheese, vegetables, and sometimes meat. The crust can be made by hand, which in days past was the test of a fine cook. Today it is much easier to buy a package of strudel phyllo. Below is a recipe for *lakror.*

Lakror me Spinaq (Lakror with Spinach and Cheese)

Filling:

1 pound spinach

2 pounds small curd cottage cheese

1 package (3 oz.) cream cheese (optional)

¾ lb. of the best feta cheese or Bulgarian cheese

6 eggs, beaten

¼ cup milk

4 tablespoons butter, melted

½ teaspoon salt

1 package frozen phyllo dough

Wash, drain, and cut up the spinach (remove stems). Steam over very low heat until tender.

Remove the spinach from the heat and drain well. Set aside to cool. Combine the cottage cheese, cream cheese, eggs, milk, butter and salt; blend well. Stir in spinach.

Cut phyllo dough to fit the pan. Butter pan. Place half of the thin sheets of the dough in pan, brushing each one with butter. Spoon in filling. Place remaining half of sheets of dough on top, brushing each one with butter. Sprinkle top generously with melted butter.

Bake at 400° for about 45 minutes or until bottom and top crusts are golden brown.

Figure 12. Lakror. Photo by Frances Trix.

For a main course, lamb is the traditional meat of Albanian cooking and the main fare of holiday meals. Lamb is roasted, prepared on skewers, or baked. Lamb casseroles and stews include various vegetables like onions, spinach, leeks, okra, parsley, and cabbage. The following recipe is an example of a dinner dish with lamb.

Mish me Lakër (Lamb Stew with Cabbage)

2–3 pounds lamb stew meat

1 medium size cabbage, cut in wedges

1 onion (chopped)

3 tablespoons butter

3–4 cups water

1 can tomato sauce (8 oz.)

½ teaspoon crushed hot pepper

salt and pepper to taste

Sauté lamb in butter until brown. Add onion and sauté until onion is transparent. Add water, tomato sauce, salt and pepper and simmer until meat is tender, approximately two hours.

Remove lamb and add cabbage. Place lamb on top of cabbage, sprinkle with crushed hot pepper and cover. Simmer slowly for 30 minutes or until the meat and cabbage are tender.

There are many delicious Albanian desserts, including rice pudding, custards, cookies known as *kurabie*, walnut cakes, sponge cakes, confections like *lokume, revani,* and *halve,* as well as famous pastries like baklava and *kadaif.* Most of these can also be found in Greek and Turkish cooking. But a more distinctive food is a sort of fried dough, like a fritter or a doughnut only lighter, known as *petulla.* It is sweet fried dough that is made and served to guests in celebration a few days after a new baby is born, or at other times as a treat. The following recipe is for *petulla.*

Petulla (Albanian Fried Dough)

2 cups flour
dash of salt
1 package dry yeast
¼ cup warm water
1 cup warm water
1 quart of oil for frying (corn oil)

Dissolve yeast in ¼ cup of warm water. Place dry ingredients in a bowl; add 1 cup warm water and yeast mixture. Mix well with wooden spoon. Soft dough will form and batter should drop easily from spoon. Set aside in a warm place to rise for 1 hour.

Heat oil in a large frying pan to 375°. Drop a tablespoon of batter into hot oil; fry 4 minutes turning once until light brown. Use a slotted spoon to remove from oil. Place on paper towels to absorb excess oil.

When guests come to visit, coffee is often served in small cups. This is a custom that is found throughout the eastern Mediterranean region. This coffee is specially made in a pure brass pot—called a *xhezve* in Albanian—a Turkish coffee pot that is a small pot with a long handle. The following is a description for making three demitasse cups of this coffee. In contrast to this recipe, during condolence visits bitter coffee may be served.

Albanian Coffee

1 cup water (8 oz.)

3 teaspoons sugar

3 teaspoons finely pulverized coffee (Turkish coffee)

Bring water, sugar and coffee to a boil, stirring constantly. Remove from the heat; skim off foam, placing a little of the foam in each cup. Return to heat and bring to a second boil. Remove from heat and pour into demitasse cup.

People who would like to sample Albanian cooking in Michigan can find it at summer ethnic festivals, like the one sponsored by the Albanian Knights of Columbus Council in Warren, Michigan, or in booths at the gatherings of Wayne State University Student Organizations, including the Albanian American Student Organization.

Albanian Language

The Albanian language is an old Indo-European language for which no other closely related languages exist. It is deeply treasured by Albanians as the major symbol of their culture and history, and as a sign of their commonality, despite their dispersal in Albania, Montenegro, Kosova, Macedonia, Greece, Italy, and most recently, Switzerland, Germany, Belgium, Canada, the United States, and Australia. The tenacity with which Albanian communities held to their language is truly remarkable. For example, in the fifteenth century when the Ottoman Empire took over their lands, some Albanians fled to Italy and Greece where they preserved their language for five hundred years. Of course, with preservation of their language there was also preservation of much of their cultural ways as well.

There are two major dialects of Albanian: the northern or Geg dialect, and the southern or Tosk dialect. These dialects are mutually understandable but there are obvious differences. In America and in Michigan, the earlier Albanian immigrants were all Tosk speakers from southern Albania, while most of the most recent Albanian immigrants, from Kosova and Montenegro, are Geg speakers.

As for the written language, Albanian has been written in three different scripts: Greek, Arabic, and Latin. Writing systems often follow religion. Thus, before the twentieth century, writing Albanian in Greek letters was associated with Orthodox Christian Albanians; writing Albanian in Arabic letters was associated with Muslim Albanians; and writing Albanian in Latin letters was associated with Roman Catholic Albanians. In the late nineteenth century, however, there was a movement for Albanian unity across religions and a special largely Latin alphabet was used by patriots who were both Muslim and Christian. A special congress, known as the Congress of Monastir after the city in which it was held, met in 1908 to decide once and for all the question of a standard alphabet for Albanian. (This city is now known as Bitola, found in today's state of Macedonia.) Delegates came to this Congress from all over the Albanian diaspora, including a representative from the Albanian American community in Boston. The delegates immediately agreed that the alphabet should use Latin letters. But there were still two different Latin alphabets to choose from. The Congress ended up supporting both alphabets, but in time, the Bashkimi or northern alphabet that used digraphs—that is, two letters to represent one sound (like "sh" or "th" in English, that each represent one sound, but have an "h" to distinguish them from "s" or "t")—became the standard Albanian alphabet for most uses.

Unlike English spelling, Albanian spelling is more directly related to pronunciation. For American English speakers to pronounce Albanian from Albanian writing, they need to note that:

- [j] is pronounced like our "y"
- [ç] is pronounced "ch,"
- [ë] is like our "uh"
- [dh] is pronounced like the first sound of "the" in English

In the common Albanian words and expressions listed below, the italicized syllable should be stressed. I have also given the pronunciation in the northern dialect as that is the dialect of most of the recent immigrants to Michigan.

Basic Words and Common Expressions in Albanian

ENGLISH	ALBANIAN	PRONUNCIATION
Simple words		
yes	po	poh
no	jo	yoh
good, okay	mirë	meer
bad	keq	kehch
so-so	ashtu ashtu	ahsh-tu ahsh-tu
Foods		
tea	çaj	chay
coffee	kafe	*kah*-veh
milk	qumësht	*chu*-musht
sugar	sheqer	sheh-*kyer*
soup	supë	*sou*-peh
meat	mish	meesh
salt	krip	kreep
Simple questions and responses		
How are you?	Si jeni?	*si* yeni?
Fine.	Mirë.	meer
Where are you from?	Nga jeni juve?	n*ga* yeni yuveh?
from Prishtina	nga Prishtinë	nga prish*teen*
from Michigan	nga Michigan	nga mih-shi-gan
Come in (welcome)	Mirë se erdhet	meer seh *er*-thet
It's good to be here.	Mirë se ju gjetëm.	meer seh yu *gye*-tem
Thank you.	Falëmnderit.	fa-lum-*nder*-it
You're welcome	S'ka për se	*ska* pur seh
good-bye (good day)	diten e mirë	*deet*en eh meer
good to see you	mirë u pafshim	meer u *pav*shim
Numbers		
1	një	nyeh
2	dy	**deu** *(say "eu" and round lips)*
3	tre	treh

4	katër	*ka*-ter
5	pes	pes
6	gjashtë	jasht
7	shtatë	shtat
8	tetë	tet
9	nënd	nund
10	dhjetë	the-yet

Poetry in Albanian is also highly respected. There is even a special name for poems and songs that are written by Albanians far from home, who miss their families and earlier homes. These are called poems or songs of *gurbet*. Many of these are written by immigrants or people who, for reasons of work or politics, have had to leave home. The following poem was written by an Albanian American, Xhevat Kallajxhi, who had to leave Albania for political reasons at the end of World War II. He settled in the United States near Washington, D.C. and used to visit Baba Rexheb at the Bektashi Teqe in Michigan every summer. This poem speaks of his love of his language and its importance to Albanian communities far from Southeast Europe.

Gjuha Jonë

Kur këndon bilbili
Herët në mëngjez
Mbi degë trandafili
Shpirtin m'a magjeps.

Këngën fort ja dua
Zëmren ma gëzon,
Se më duket mua
Sikur shqip këndon.

Gjuha jon' amtare
S'ka shoqe në botë.
Esht' e bukur fare
Nga ç'do gjë që thotë.

Prandaj s'do lejuar
Të humbasë kot.
Ky thesar i çmuar
Se s'e gjejmë dot.

Our Language

When the nightingale sings
Early in the morning
From the branch of the rose bush
I am enchanted.

I want it to sing and sing;
It lifts my heart so,
It is as if it sings
Albanian to me.

Our mother tongue
Has no friends in the world.
Still it is as beautiful
As anything that is spoken.

That is why it should not be allowed
Ever to be lost.
For this precious treasure
We would never find again.

Albanian Music

Suzanne Camino

Albanian music is comprised of a remarkable variety of styles, songs, and instruments. Although the listening tastes of Albanians range from the latest popular music of the Middle East and the West, to classical music by Albanian and Western composers, the pride of many Albanians is undoubtedly the vast and rich repertoire of Albanian traditional music. This repertoire encompasses both instrumental and vocal styles and differs greatly according to region and ethnic group.

Music plays an important role in the lives of Albanian communities both in Southeast Europe and abroad. Traditionally, special songs accompanied every important holiday and life cycle event including baptisms, circumcisions, weddings, and funerals; many of these songs continue to play an important role in the celebrations of Albanians in the United States.

For Albanian communities all over the world, the event which features the most exuberant music making and in which Albanians take the greatest pleasure is the Albanian wedding. For many Albanians, weddings are the most important manifestations and celebrations of Albanian culture; the music and traditions which are performed at weddings remind the community of its special Albanian identity. Albanians of every region have their own songs for each point of the wedding ritual, including songs that the groom's family sings when escorting the bride from her parents' home, and songs that describe the beauty and good character of the bride and her sorrow upon leaving her family.

The evening reception that follows a wedding will usually feature a band made up of one or two singers, a keyboard or accordion player, a drummer, and a clarinetist. The band provides music for dancing, often playing for hours without a break. The musicians are usually quite versatile and will play both traditional and modern instruments over the course of the evening. The drummer, for example, may play both a drum set and a *daulle*, a two-headed drum which is carried in front of the body and played with two different-sized sticks.

The best occasions to hear live Albanian music in Michigan, apart from weddings, are at Albanian religious and community festivals, concerts, and patriotic celebrations such as the Albanian Flag Day on November 28th. At such events, the joyous musical atmosphere of an Albanian wedding is recreated and celebrated in song and dance, and the community's favorite songs are sung, including wedding songs, humorous songs, patriotic songs, and love songs.

Figure 13. Young Albanian men in ethnic garb for Albanian Independence Day in Michigan. Photo by Mark P. Gjokaj.

Albanian music varies from region to region, with the most marked differences being between the north and south. Albanians from Montenegro, the northern region of Albania, northern Macedonia, and Kosova (known as Gegs) are famous for their heroic ballads, which are often accompanied by a stringed instrument such as the *çiftëli*, (*cheeftel-ee*) a small, long-necked lute with two strings, or the *lahuta* (la-*oo*-tah) a larger lute which is played with a small bow. These ballads, which often tell of important battles, heroic deeds and other historical events, were traditionally sung and played by men, but are now being learned and performed by women and girls as well among the Albanians of the United States. Women of the northern regions may also sing to the accompaniment of the *dajre*, a large frame drum which resembles a tambourine, or the *tepsia* (tep-*see*-ah) a round, copper baking pan which is spun on end and struck with the hand. The singer directs her voice into the *tepsia* as it rapidly turns, and the sound of her singing is transformed by the vibrating air surrounding the spinning pan.

Albanians from the south (known as Tosks) often perform songs in small community and family groups. These choral songs are described as polyphonic (*polifonik*) because they are made up of several different lines of melody, which are sung simultaneously. Albanian polyphonic songs are most often performed without instrumental accompaniment. The leader, or first soloist of the song will begin singing and is soon joined by the second (and sometimes the third and fourth) solo lines. The last voices to enter are those of the drone (*iso*). Any number of singers may participate in singing the drone part, which is sung on a single pitch. In this way everyone present can participate and support the solo singers.

Another genre of Albanian song is the serenade (*serenata*), a type of love song which comes from the southeastern Albanian city of Korçe. Michigan is the new home to many Albanians from Korçe who have fond memories of young men strolling the streets with guitars to play as they sing serenades under the windows of the young women of the town. Serenades are now sung by both men and women. A leading exponent of the serenade is the famous Albanian singer Ermira Babali, who now resides in Michigan where she continues to perform and to organize Albanian cultural events.

Figure 14. Ermira Babali, Albanian singer who now lives in Sterling Heights, Michigan, performing for Flag Day Celebration, 1999. Photo by Suzanne Camino.

Many Albanian musicians who have emigrated in recent years to Michigan have enriched the musical landscape of the state. Some are gifted amateurs who grew up playing and singing music for family and community events; others, like Ermira Babali of the Korçe district and Bukurijë Domi, of the Prespa region in Macedonia, are Albanian radio and television stars who continue to perform for their communities. Still others are conservatory-trained classical musicians who left behind jobs in the Albanian national opera and orchestra.

Some Albanian musicians in the United States are making attempts to marry Albanian folk music to other musical traditions. One such musician is Djeto Juncaj of the Detroit band, The Immigrant Suns. He is a *çifteli* and accordion player who unites the old-world sounds of Albanian and other traditional musics with new American alternative music.

While Albanian traditional music possesses many distinctive features, listeners to the music of other Balkan traditions might recognize some affinity between the music of Albanian urban ensembles, and urban Greek and Turkish music. Fans of singing groups such as the Bulgarian State Women's Chorus will find much to enjoy in the complex and powerful sounds of Albanian polyphonic singing. Of course, the beauty of Albanian music, like that of any musical tradition, cannot be adequately described in words and must be heard to be enjoyed. Fortunately, many high-quality commercial recordings of Albanian music have recently been released, and interested listeners can at last hear for themselves an amazing repertoire that until recently was largely unknown to those outside the Albanian community.

Discography

The following recordings of Albanian music are available on CD and may be ordered through most media retailers:

Anthology of World Music: Music from Albania. Rounder Records Corp., 1999. Rounder CD 5151.

Albania, Vocal and Instrumental Polyphony. Recorded by Bernard Lortat-Jacob with Benjamin Kruta. France: Le Chant du Monde, 1988. LDX 274897.

Cold Water, Dry Stone: New Music from Traditional Sources. Music of Evan Chambers performed by Quorum. Albany Records, 2000.

Cry You Mountains, Cry You Fields. Saydisc Records, England, 1999. CD-SDL 431.

Famille Lela de Përmet: Polyphonies vocales et instrumentales d'Albanie. Produced by Yorrick Benoist and Claude Chaigneau. One compact disc. Label Bleu LBLC 2503/Harmonia Mundi HM 83.

Folk Music of Albania. Recorded and edited by A. L. Lloyd. London: Topic Records, 1994. TSCD904.

L'Albanie mysteriueuse. Compiled and with notes by Marcel Cellier. One compact disc. Disques Pierre Verany PV 750010.

Laverbariu:Songs from the City of Roses. Recorded by Ben Mandelson. U.K.:Ace Records, 1995. CDORBD 091 1995.

Montenegro. The Immigrant Suns. Pho-ne-tic Records, 1994. SKR 1545

Vocal Traditions of Albania. England: Saydisc, 1997. CD-SDL 421.

Notes

1. The analogy of the Albanians in the Balkans with the Scots in the British Isles is valid on several grounds. As mentioned above, both were earlier inhabitants of their regions who were pushed into less desirable lands by more numerous people who came later; the Scots were pushed north by the Anglo Saxons, while the Albanians were pushed west by the Slavs. Thus both came to live in mountainous terrain. Both peoples became known for their skill and courage as soldiers, partly because in order to survive as minorities they had to assert themselves. But they also became soldiers because their lands were not rich enough to support them by farming. Both have highly developed clan systems. And both rebelled at different times in their histories.

    The analogy is not only the work of scholars and observers. Kosovar refugees in Detroit reported to me that one of the most popular films in the 1990s in Prishtina was *Braveheart* the powerful story of Sir William Wallace, a Scots leader of the thirteenth century who fought the English and was eventually captured and executed. The Kosovars reportedly watched *Braveheart* many times, recognizing it as "our story too."

2. Shemseddin Sami Bey (Frashëri), a Muslim Albanian from southern Albania, wrote the finest dictionary of Ottoman Turkish, in Istanbul in the late nineteenth century. In Albanian history, his brothers are also well

known: Naim Frashëri—the great nineteenth-century Albanian poet, and Abdul Frashëri—the politician who was a driving force behind the League of Prizren that first brought Muslim and Christian Albanians together for defense of their lands in 1878.

3. Mother Teresa was born Agnes Gonxha Bojaxhi to Albanian parents in Shkopje, in Macedonia. Her family came from Prizren, in Kosova. Both Macedonia and Kosova included significant Albanian populations that were left outside Albania proper when the Great Powers drew boundary lines in 1913 and 1918. More specifically, most sources note that over half of the Albanians were left outside of Albania by these decisions. (For more information on Mother Teresa, see the excellent works on her by Lush Gjerjgi, brother of Father Ndue Gjergji of Our Lady of the Albanians.)

4. In Massachusetts a Greek Orthodox priest not only refused to bury an Orthodox Christian Albanian who had engaged in Albanian nationalist activities, he also stopped other Orthodox priests from burying him. This event precipitated the founding of the Albanian Orthodox Church in 1908 in America.

5. The Bektashis were one of the two main Sufi Orders of the Ottoman Empire, the other being the better known Mevlevi or "whirling dervishes." The Bektashis were founded in the thirteenth century in Anatolia and spread with Ottoman armies to the Balkans in the fifteenth century. By the late nineteenth century, Albanians held leadership positions among the Bektashi in Turkey. In Albania, the Bektashis, who had always been known for their tolerance of different religions, played an important symbolic and practical role in the movement for Albanian independence from Ottoman Turkey. When Ataturk closed all the Sufi Orders in Turkey, the Bektashis moved their headquarters to Tirana, capital of Albania.

6. Yugoslavia included six republics: Slovenia, Croatia, Serbia, Bosnia, Monte-negro, and Macedonia until its disintegration in the early 1990s. At that time first Slovenia, then Croatia, Bosnia, and Macedonia all declared their independence from Yugoslavia. This left only the two republics of Serbia and Montenegro still included in Yugoslavia.

The larger, six-republic country of Yugoslavia before 1991 is sometimes referred to as "former Yugoslavia," to distinguish it from the smaller two republic country that also uses the name "Yugoslavia." Kosova is a south-ern region that was incorporated into Serbia in 1918. Its large Albanian population sets it off from the rest of Serbia. From 1974 to 1989 it had special status as an autonomous province. As will be discussed in chapter five, this special status was revoked in 1989. Before this time, many Kosovar Albanians wanted republic status in Yugoslavia for their region, that is, to no longer be considered part of Serbia. Since 1989, and especially after the expulsions of 1999, Kosovar Albanians want independence of their region from Yugoslavia.

7. Personal communication from Father Ndrevashaj, long time priest to the Detroit Albanian Catholic community, and previously papal representative in charge of assisting immigration of Catholics from the Balkans.

8. *The Detroit Free Press* (29 April 1991) noted 55,000 Albanians in Michigan, a figure quoted from a speech of a prominent Michigan Albanian leader, Ekrem Bardha, in an earlier *Detroit Free Press* article of 15 March 1991. Corroboration of these higher estimates comes from people familiar with the Hamtramck area and the recent immigrants from Kosova and Montenegro.

9. These Detroit Muslims contributed to the publication of the Orthodox Christian prayer book as members of Vatra and in honor of the Muslim, Faik Konitza, deceased co-founder of Vatra.

10. "The Consecration of St. Thomas Orthodox Church: Albanian Archdiocese, Orthodox Church in America, Farmington Hills, Michigan, 14 October 1989," (consecration service and souvenir journal). See the section on the history of St. Thomas, compiled by Victor Chacho.

11. These guests were G. Mennen Williams, Governor of the state of Michigan; Eugene Van Antwerp, Mayor of the city of Detroit; George Edwards, president of the Detroit City Council; and Hicks Griffiths, State Chairman of the Democratic Committee. Such a guest list does not indicate work of people with only four years of political experience. Rather, I see this ability to reach top political leaders as building on Albanians' political experience with Vatra from earlier years.

12. The earliest Albanian Muslim Society in America was founded in Biddeford, Maine, in 1915 (Thernstrom, 1980:26). But this community did not continue; it appears that they did not consecrate or build a mosque.

13. "Baba" means "father," and also signifies "head of a teqe" among the Bektashi. It was only with the opening of the teqe that Dervish Rexheb became Baba Rexheb.

14. There is no comparable institution in Christianity. Some have likened the Muslim Orders to Masonic Lodges in that they include people who have gone through private initiation yet remain living in the lay community. But in contrast to Masonic Lodges, the Muslim Orders also have full-time clerics, more like "monks."

15. Lazar Hila, who sponsored Prenk Gruda, had settled in Detroit. He helped Baba Rexheb of the Teqe with gardening, and interestingly enough, lived out his final days at the Teqe.

16. He sponsored over 700 people, largely of the Gruda clan. For this great service his name, which was Prenk Stanaj, was changed to Prenk Gruda.

17. The Albanian Orthodox church found itself in a delicate position because it is a member of a local Orthodox Council that also includes Serbs. It met this by deciding to donate $1,000 to Albanian refugees and $1,000 to Serbian refugees as well. On the national level, the Albanian Orthodox Archdiocese contributed $150,000 for Kosova relief.

18. According to its web site, NAAC also "seeks to persuade the White House, Congress, foreign policy experts, the media, and the American people that the United States can and should exert leadership in helping address the plight of Albanians and thereby securing peace and stability in the Balkans. In particular NAAC seeks political, economic, and military support for the Republic of Albania; support for the self-determination of the people of Kosova; full participation and representation of the ethnic Albanians in Macedonia, as well as full minority rights wherever the Albanians are not a majority. NAAC is also dedicated to involving Albanian Americans in the political processes here at home . . . NAAC receives financial assistance primarily from individual Albanian Americans. It does not receive funding or direction from foreign government" (*www.naac.org: homepage*).

References and Suggested Sources

The most highly recommended in each category are starred.

Albanians in America

Demo, Constantine A. *The Albanians in America: the First Arrivals* (in English and Albanian). Boston: Fatbardhësia of Katundi, 1960.

*Federal Writers' Project. *The Albanian Struggle in the Old World and New.* New York: AMS Press (originally published in 1939, Boston: The Writer, Inc.), 1975.

Gruda, Prenk. *Ditari i nji Zemrës së Lëndueme (Diary of a Wounded Heart) 1937–1975.* Detroit, n.p. 1985.

Kallajxhi, Xhevat. *Bektashizmi dhe Teqeja Shqiptare N'Amerikë* (Bektashism and the Albanian Teqe in America). Detroit: Teqe, 1964.

Nagi, Dennis L. *The Albanian-American Odyssey: A Pilot Study of the Albanian Community of Boston, Massachusetts.* New York: AMS Press, 1989.

Thernstrom, Stephan. "Albanians." In *Harvard Encyclopedia of American Ethnic Groups.* Cambridge, Mass.: Belknap Press, 1980: 23–28.

Trix, Frances. *Spiritual Discourse: Learning with an Islamic Master.* Philadelphia: University of Pennsylvania Press, 1993.

———. "Bektashi Tekke and Sunni Mosque of Albanian Muslims in America." In *Muslim Communities in the United States.* Albany: State University of New York Press, 1994. 359–80.

———. "Blessing Cars: A Classic Sufi Play on Ritual in Immigrant America." *Journal of Ritual Studies* 10, no. 2 (1997): 109–30.

History and Current Portrait of Albanians in Southeast Europe

*Durham, Mary Edith. *High Albania*. New York: Arno Press (reprinted 1971), 1909.

———. *Twenty Years of Balkan Tangle*. London: George Allen & Unwin, 1920.

Hall, Derek. *Albania and Albanians*. New York: St. Martins, 1994.

Jacques, Edwin. *The Albanians: An Ethnic History from Prehistoric Times to the Present*. Jefferson, N.C.: McFarland & Co., 1995.

Sarner, Harvey. *Rescue in Albania: One Hundred Percent of Jews in Albania Rescued from Holocaust*. Cathedral City, Calif.: Brunswick Press, 1997.

*Sherer, Stan (photographer) and Marjorie Senechal. *Long Life to Your Children: A Portrait of High Albania*. Amherst: University of Massachusetts Press, 1995.

*Skendi, Stavro. *The Albanian National Awakening: 1878–1912*. Princeton: Princeton University Press, 1967.

Trix, Frances. "Alphabet Conflict in the Balkans: Albanian and the Congress of Monastir." *The International Journal of the Sociology of Language* 128 (1997) 1–24.

Vickers, Miranda. *Albania: A Modern History*. London: I. B. Tauris, 1995.

Albanian Art, Dance, Folklore, Literature, Music, Religion, Cuisine

Elsie, Robert. *Albanian Folktales and Legends*. Tirana: Naim Frasheri Publishing, 1994.

———. *Studies in Modern Albanian Literature and Culture*. Boulder: East European Monographs, distributed by Columbia University Press, 1996.

Fox, Leonard (translator). *Kanuni i Lekë Dukagjinit: The Code of Lekë Dukagjinit* (in Albanian and English). New York: Gjonlekaj, 1989.

*Gjergji, Lush. *Mother Teresa: Her Life, Her Works*. New York: New City Press, 1991.

———. *Mother Teresa: To Live, To Love, To Witness Her Spiritual Way*. New York: New City Press, 1998.

Goçi, Rexhep. *Gjerqj Kastrioti-Skenderbeu në antet figurative* ("George Kastrioti-Skenderbeg in Figurative Art"). Prishtinë, Kosova, 1998.

Grup aut (a group of authors). *Arti Bashkohor i Kosovës* ("Contemporary Art of Kosova"). Prishtinë, Kosova, 1988.

Hysa, Klementina and Ramazan John Hysa. *The Best of Albanian Cooking: Favorite Family Recipes.* New York: Hippocrene Press, 1998.

*Kadare, Ismail. *Chronicle in Stone.* New York: The Meredith Press, 1987.

————. *Doruntine.* New York: New Amsterdam Books, 1988.

*————. *The General of the Dead Army.* New York: New Amsterdam, 1991.

————. *Broken April.* New York: New Amsterdam Books, 1990. [Kadare is the foremost Albanian writer; many of his works are translated in English]

Noli, Fan S. *Historia e Skënderbeut* (The Story of Skenderbey). Boston: Federata Pan-Shqiptare Vatra, 1950.

*Reineck, Janet. "The Place of the Dance Event in Social Organization and Social Change among Albanians in Kosovo, Yugoslavia." *UCLA Journal of Dance Ethnology* 10 (1986): 27–38.

*Sugarman, Jane C. *Engendering Song: Singing and Subjectivity at Prespa Albanian Weddings.* Chicago: University of Chicago Press, 1997.

Women's Guild of St. Mary's Albanian Orthodox Church. *Albanian Cookbook.* Worcester, Mass.: St. Mary's Albanian Orthodox Church, 1977.

Zendani, Abdulmexhid (translated by Imam Shuajb Gërguri). *Mrekullia Shkencore në Kur'an dhe Sunnet* ("The Scientific Miracles in the Qur'an and the Sunna"). Harper Woods, Mich.: Albanian Islamic Center, 1999.

Focus on Kosova, its Past and Recent History of the Crisis.

Cohen, Roberta and David A. Korn. "Failing the Internally Displaced." *Forced Migration Review,* theme issue on Learning from Kosovo 5 (1999): 11–13.

De Vries, Franklin (ed.). *Kosovo: The conflict between the Serbs and the Albanians and the role of the international community.* Antwerp: IPIS, 1995.

*Elsie, Robert (ed.). *Kosovo: In the Heart of the Powder Keg.* Boulder: East European Monographs, no. CDLXXVII [Includes important twentieth century historical texts and commentaries on Kosovo by Kosovar Albanian leaders (Qosja, Demaci, Bukoshi, Rugova, Vinca) all well translated into English], 1997.

Human Rights Watch/Helsinki. *Human Rights Abuses in Kosovo.* New York: Human Rights Watch, 1994, 1998.

*Malcolm, Noel. *Kosovo: A Short History.* New York: New York University Press, 1998.

*Mead, Alice. *Adem's Cross.* New York: Bantam Doubleday of Dell, 1998. [book for young adults]

Mertus, Julie. *Kosovo: How Myths and Truths Started a War.* Berkeley: University of California Press, 1999.

Reineck, Janet. *The Past as Refuge: Gender, Migration and Ideology among the Kosova Albanians.* unpublished dissertation in anthropology from the University of California at Berkeley, 1991.

Trix, Frances. "Publishing in Kosovo: Focus on Kosovar Albanians." *Journal of Slavic and East European Information Resources* 1, nos. 2–3 (2000):159–83.

———. "Reframing the Forced Migration and Rapid Return of Kosovar Albanians." In Elzbieta Gozdziak and Dianna Shandy (eds.) *Selected Papers on Refugees and Immigrants* 8, American Anthropological Association (2000):250–75.

Vickers, Miranda. *Between Albanian and Serb: a Study of Kosovo.* London: Hurst & Co., 1998.

Booklets, Albums, Reviews, and Newspapers

Albanian Catholic Information Center. *Albanian Catholic Bulletin (Buletini Katolik Shqiptar).* published annually by the Albanian Catholic Information Center, Santa Clara, Calif., 1988, 1989.

Albanian Orthodox Church. *Fiftieth Anniversary Book of the Albanian Orthodox Church in America 1908–1958.* Boston: Albanian Orthodox Church in America, comp. 1960.

American Moslem Society. *Albanian Moslem Congress Review (Rivista e Kongresit Mysliman Shqiptar).* Detroit, Michigan, 1947.

American Moslem Society. *Jeta Muslimane Shqiptare (The Albanian Moslem Life).* Imam Vehbi Ismail (ed). Detroit: Albanian American Moslem Society, 1949, 1950.

Sterling Heights Ethnic Issues Advisory Committee. "Getting to Know your Albanian-American Neighbors." Sterling Heights, Mich.: City of Sterling Heights, 1992.

Illyria. Published in Albanian and English. New York: Ekrem Publications, 1991-present. [The foremost Albanian American newspaper since the mid-1990s.]

Rexhebi, Baba. *Zëri Bektashizmes The Voice of Bektashism* 1, no. 2. (1955). Detroit: Komisionit të Teqes.

Vatra. *Albumi Dyzetvjeçar në Amerikë: 1906–1946 i Hirësisë Tij Peshkop Fan S. Noli* (The Album of the Forty Years in America of His Holiness Archbishop Fan S. Noli). Boston: Federata Vatra, 1948.

CDs of Albanian Music

For recommended CDs of Albanian music, see the list of Discography at the end of the section on Albanian Music.

Web Sites/Internet

www.albanian.com. Note it is "Albanian," not "Albania" to encompass Albanians who live in different countries.

www.alb-net.com. The content is political events affecting Albanians.

www.aano.org. This is the web site of the Albanian American National Organization, founded in 1946.

www.frosina.org. This well organized site puts out information on Albanian culture and history. It also serves as a resource for Albanian immigrants. The Frosina Foundation was founded by Albanian American Van Christo in Boston, and is named after his Albanian mother.

www. naac.org. This is the web site of the National Albanian American Council, the primary lobbying group in Washington DC for Albanian issues, particularly those relating to foreign policy, founded in 1996.

Index

A

AANO (Albanian American National Organization), 41

Albania: background to emigration; 8–10; during Communist times, 19; in the 1990s; relief to, 40; problems of, 42; dialects of, 51; music of, 57

Albanian Aid Society, 40

Albanian American Bektashi Teqe. *See* Bektashi Teqe

Albanian American Moslem Society, 21, 23

Albanian American Student Association, 32, 49

Albanian Islamic Center, 22, 34, 39

Albanian Orthodox Church, 4, 62n. 4

Albanian Society of Orthodox Christians, 21

Ali, Orhan, 8

Athanas, Anthony, 45

B

Baba Rexheb: early founding of teqe, 5, 23; passing of, 24; honoring of, 43; title of, 63n. 13

Babali, Ermira, 57, 58

Bajraktari, Hajdar, 41

Balli Kombëtar (National Front), 9

Bardha, Ekrem, 14, 41, 63

Bektashi Teqe (Taylor, Mich.), 5–6, 23–24, 42

besa (Albanian pledge of honor), 1

Black, Julie, 41

Bojaxhi, Agnes Gonxha, 62. *See* Mother Teresa

Boston, 4, 5, 7, 45, 52

Broomfield, William (Michigan Congressman), 40

C

Camaj, Dom Prenk, 26

Catholic Archdiocese of Detroit, 32, 33–34

Chacho, Victor, 63n. 10

Chicago, 18, 38
Clement XI, 2
Congress of Monastir, 52

D

Dearborn (Mich.), 17, 41
Detroit: early immigration to, 5, 7–9,
    11–12; Christian-Muslim coop-
    eration in, 14; current residence
    in, 17; as center for religious
    institutions, 21–23, 25–26; as
    center of Kosova relief, 32–34;
    contributions to, 38–39; in terms
    of other Albanian communities
    in America, 42
Diocletian, 2
Domi, Bukurijë, 58
Durrës, 24

E

Episcopal Cathedral of Detroit:
    Episcopal Refugee Relief, 32, 33

F

Fico, Agron, 28
Frashëri Brothers: Shemseddin
    Sami, 61n. 2; Abdul and Naim,
    62.n 2

G

Geg (northern Albanian people), 51;
    their dialect, 51, 57
Gegaj, Gjevalin, 40
Gellçi, Thoma and Diana, 28
Gërguri, Imam Shuajb, 22
Gjakova (Kosova), 26
Gjergji, Father Ndue, 26, 62n. 3
Gjirokastër (Albania), 4
Gjokaj, Mark P., 16, 19, 25, 40
Goçi, Rexhep, 34, 35
Gruda, Prenk, 25, 64n. 15

H

Hackensack (N.J.), 18
Hamtramck (Mich.), 17, 33, 39, 63
Harper Woods (Mich.), 22, 34
Hila, Lazar, 64
Hoxha, Enver, 27, 28, 42

I

Illyria (newspaper), 12, 41
Illyrians, 1
Imam Vehbi Ismail, 21, 39
Immigrant Suns, 58, 59
Ismail, Imam Vehbi. *See* Imam
    Vehbi
Ivezaj, Pjetër, 39

J

Jewish Family Services of Southfield
    (Mich.), 32, 33
Jews, 1, 18, 33, 43
Juncaj, Djeto, 58

K

Kadare, Ismail, 2
Kallajxhi, Xhevat, 14, 54
Kastrioti, Gjergji, 2, *See* Skenderbeg
Kçira, Father Anton, 26
KLA (Kosova Liberation Army), 31
Konitza, Faik, 13, 63
Korçe, 4, 7, 8, 57, 58
Kosova: source of immigration,
    9–10, 12, 24; oppression in, 27,
    28–32; refugees from, 34–35;
    assistance to, 40; refugee distri-
    bution from, 43; situation in
    Yugoslavia 62–63n .6; NAAC pol-
    icy on, 64n. 18

L

League of Prizren, 13, 62
Legalitet (Royalist Party), 9
Liolin, Father Nicholas, 38

Lutheran Immigrant and Refugee
  Services of Detroit, 32, 33

M

Macedonia: source of immigration,
  9, 10; Prespa, 24; refugees in, 32,
  43; alphabet congress in, 52;
  music in, 57, 58, birth place of
  Mother Teresa, 62; NAAC policy
  on 64n. 18
Milosevic, Slobodan, 2, 27, 29, 30,
  31
Montenegro: source of Catholic
  Albanians, 5, 9–10, 12, 24–25, as
  host of refugees, 43, music in 57
Moslem-American Society, 5
Mother Teresa, 2, 3, 40, 62

N

NAAC (National Albanian American
  Congress), 41, 64
NATO, 2, 31, 32, 43
Ndrevashaj, Dom Prenk, 25, 63
New York, 4, 5, 12, 25, 31, 39, 41
Noli, Fan (Archbishop Theofan), 4,
  13, 14

O

Operation Provide Rescue, 32
Ottoman Empire, 1, 8, 13, 62
Our Lady of the Albanians (Beverly
  Hills, Mich.), 25, 26, 32, 62

P

Peppo, Ted, 7
Presidency of the Albanian Muslim
  Community in the United States
  and Canada, 39
Prespa (Macedonia), 9, 24, 58
Prishtina (Kosova), 22, 26, 29, 31,
  39, 61n. 1

R

Rakipi, Afërdita, 41
Repishti, Sami, 41
Rexheb, Baba. *See* Baba Rexheb
Rosso, Sandi, 33, 34
Rugova, Ibrahim, 31

S

Selimaj, Bruno, 45
Shahin, Shije Orhan, 45
Shkalla, Baba Flamur, 24
Shkodër (Albania), 21
Skenderbeg (in Albanian,
  Skënderbeu), 2
St. Andrew's Episcopal Church
  (Ann Arbor, Mich.), 35
St. Anthony's Bread, 40
St. Mary's College (Orchard Lake,
  Mich.), 28
St. Paul's Albanian Catholic Church
  (Warren, Mich.), 26, 32
St. Thomas Orthodox Church
  (Farmington Hills, Mich.), 5, 38
Stanaj, Prenk, 64.n 16. *See* Gruda
Stublla (Kosova), 26

T

Taylor (Mich.), 18, 24
Toronto (Canada), 18
Tosk (southern Albanian people),
  51; their dialect, 51, 57

V

Vatra, 4, 13, 63

W

Warren (Mich.), 26
Waterbury (Conn.), 18
Wayne State University (Detroit,
  Mich.), 28, 32, 49